Lynn —
Be about yourself!
Open to the possibilities
of 2022!
Elizabeth Owens
11-19-03

Women Celebrating Life

Attitude Is the Difference

Create in your mind a situation in your life that would be an unwelcome change. You perceive this event pessimistically.

How do you feel?

Agitated? Bitter? Angry? Fearful?

Again, envision that same change entering your life.

Now imagine yourself choosing to welcome that change. Picture yourself celebrating the transition.

Now how do you feel?

Peaceful? Curious? Empowered? Prepared?

See the difference a positive perspective can make?

Women Celebrating Life offers empowering rituals, affirmations, and nurturing suggestions for celebrating the many transitions a woman may experience in her lifetime's journey.

About the Author

Elizabeth Owens was certified as a medium in 1984 and ordained as a Spiritualist Minister in 1985. She has written and self-published four books, including *H.E.L.P.: The Spiritual Approach to Weight Loss*; *Spirit Guides: The Art of Communication*; *What You Need to Know about Spiritual Readings*; and *The Story of Cassadaga*. Her next book is *The Art of Communicating with Spirit* (Llewellyn, 2001). As a medium and psychic artist, she has appeared on television shows such as *The Other Side*, *CNN*, *Hard Copy*, *Now It Can Be Told*, and *Current Affair*, and has participated in news shows broadcast in Japan, Germany, Australia, France, England, and Florida. Currently living in Cassadaga, Florida, Elizabeth teaches spiritual development classes and presents seminars while she and her husband enjoy the continuing process of renovating their 1906 Victorian home.

To Write to the Author

If you wish to contact the author or would like more information about this book, please write to the author in care of Llewellyn Worldwide and we will forward your request. Both the author and publisher appreciate hearing from you and learning of your enjoyment of this book and how it has helped you. Llewellyn Worldwide cannot guarantee that every letter written to the author can be answered, but all will be forwarded. Please write to:

Elizabeth Owens
℅ Llewellyn Worldwide
P.O. Box 64383, Dept. K508-8
St. Paul, MN 55164-0383, U.S.A.

Please enclose a self-addressed stamped envelope for reply, or $1.00 to cover costs. If outside U.S.A., enclose international postal reply coupon.

Honoring the Passages of Life

A Guide to Growth & Transformation

Women Celebrating Life

Elizabeth Owens

2000
Llewellyn Publications
St. Paul, Minnesota 55164-0383, U.S.A.

First Edition
First Printing, 2000

Book design and editing by Rebecca Zins
Cover art ©2000 by Wendy Froshay
Cover design by Lisa Novak
Interior illustration by Nyease Somersett

Library of Congress Cataloging-in-Publication Data
Owens, Elizabeth, 1948-
Women celebrating life: honoring the passages of life: a guide to growth & transformation / [by Elizabeth Owens].—1st ed.
p. cm.
ISBN 1-56718-508-8
1. Women—Anniversaries, etc. 2. Women—Psychology. 3. Women—Religious life. 4. Rites and ceremonies. I. Title.

HQ1206.O83 2000
305.4—dc21

00-028217

Llewellyn Publications
A Division of Llewellyn Worldwide, Ltd.
P.O. Box 64383, Dept. K508-8
St. Paul, MN 55164-0383, U.S.A.
www.llewellyn.com

 Printed in the United States of America on recycled paper

Contents

Beginnings

Healing of the Body and Heart

Pathways In Our Lives

Acknowledgments

It is with the deepest respect and most humble of attitudes that I wish to acknowledge those who have helped in the creation of this book.

Fran Ellison, for painstakingly editing my writing. Without her dedication to the work at hand and her unending encouragement, I never would have completed this book. She has been on this path with me from the very beginning, and I am deeply indebted to her.

Vincent Owens, my husband. No woman could ask for a more supportive and sensitive husband, a better friend and companion, or a more gentle soul to share her life with. I am so very grateful for all that he has contributed to my life.

Elizabeth Henderson, my mother in spirit.

Introduction: Celebration of Life

Societies have always practiced some form of ceremony. The ancients celebrated such events as the full moon, solstices, harvests, and the sowing of seed. Weddings, funerals, and baptisms are examples of other rituals that have been practiced for centuries. It is an activity that often conveys reverence, gratitude, and honor. For women today, performing a ceremony has the capacity to evoke within us self-love and positive acknowledgments. In the privacy of our homes, we can celebrate life.

It is my belief and experience that if we honor our feminine energy through ceremony, we become better acquainted with our inner Self. Through ceremony, we can heal our spirits and, in most situations, create new realities simply by choosing how we perceive events in our lives. By changing our perception, we can open ourselves to wondrous possibilities and magnificent happenings with benefits that are everlasting! Every woman can glorify all her circumstances and manifest a uniquely fulfilling existence by celebrating events in her life that perhaps she never realized were worthy of recognition. In solitude, she can perform ceremonies that will release pent-up emotions, soothe old wounds, and nurture the feminine spirit—all celebratory acts for the Self!

Everything begins with thought

My desire is that all women learn to regard and value themselves as divine beings. I wrote this book to help women of all ages gain a greater appreciation for who they truly are and who they are becoming—and how to get there from here! It is especially important that young women who are just embarking on their path begin their journey on sure feet, supported by self-assurance, self-worth, and self-appreciation. The ceremonies presented for them as well as women of all ages will assist their adventures.

As adults, we have the opportunity to evolve into stronger, wiser women when we incorporate the act of ceremony into our lives. Through ceremony, we can learn how to bring closure to situations, praise the beginnings of new ones, broaden our horizons by acknowledging our sisterhood, and open ourselves to spiritual awakenings that are yet to come.

All of us have the ability to manifest positive outcomes for our circumstances. By choosing to view all life changes as positive, natural processes, we truly can put an uplifting spin on any event; in this way we learn to celebrate life!

Today is a new day, a special one, full of hope and anticipation for bright and beautiful manifestations, glorious escapades, lusty experiences, and dreams being fulfilled. Every day blesses us with wondrous opportunities for growth. When the sun, in all her glory, lights up the morning sky, we are receiving our official notification that another day has been born. The sky is the azure backdrop to the reflection of the light within all of us, that special light of the Creator. We are being given another chance to achieve success, manifest our desires, and conquer our fears so we may attain self-empowerment and realize our full potential. This is life. We can choose to make it a grand adventure!

We speak to ourselves through our thoughts, which are very powerful. The more emotion placed behind the thought, the more potent is the energy. I am a spiritual counselor and teacher by profession. Thoughts are things is a common phrase taught in this field. Everything begins with thought. In order to construct a table, for instance, someone first had to think about it. After they saw it in their mind, they probably drew a diagram on paper, and then began to physically build the table. The thought produced the object.

Thoughts are pure energy. All action is derived from thought and is generated by emotion. The energy force follows the thought through the law of vibration. So where a thought is directed, a force will follow. Thoughts are things!

We can choose to have a positive perception about almost anything in life. If something makes us unhappy or disappointed, we have the power to change our perspective or how we perceive its effect upon us. With a little effort, we can discover the hidden possibilities within any circumstance and recognize that opportunities are abundant and new intriguing challenges are following. As an example, a friend of mine was relieved of her position due to politics within a firm. She was devastated by this but attempted to see the good within this self-perceived horrible event. Soon she realized that she had far more time available in which to create. An endeavor that had been germinating within her heart suddenly was possible to bring into fruition due to the increase in time. The new project would open untold doors for her and present her with a challenge to complete it. My friend eventually believed that the company had done her a favor by eliminating her position.

Adopting an attitude of gratitude about all events is a practice that produces surprising results. When we strive to view all circumstances as gifts for the soul, we are on the road to higher blessings. We may not be able to understand exactly why something has occurred at this time, but we can learn to trust in the process. Everything happens for a reason. Given the proper space, and by doing our part, good will eventually manifest at the perfect moment. Thank whatever you recognize as being the Spiritual Power in your life for all your circumstances.

Thank you, God, for this experience. I am learning.

The Art of Ceremony

The ceremonies in this book are intended to project positive energy into every circumstance, producing a brighter outlook and more even emotions. I have always found that a happy heart and positive thoughts attract favorable conditions. The intent in some of the rituals is to release unwanted feelings and nurture a more compassionate perspective. This begins the healing process. I also emphasize the benefits of journaling as a tool for creating new vision and facilitating healing of the soul.

Some of the ceremonies recognize very special events, such as a wedding or the anticipated arrival of a child. During these happy times it is not the purpose of the ceremony to uplift emotions or heal the spirit, but rather to celebrate the event. The ceremony will also assist in focusing, within this marvelous happening, on what is really important in life.

Instead of dreading our birthdays, we can choose to celebrate them, honoring our unique Self and bringing glory to this special day. When a woman stands at the threshold of her fiftieth year, she needs to recognize that she carries a mountain of wisdom within her bosom from the multitude of events she has experienced. Her being is enhanced because of her age. When this woman understands how truly grand she really is, she will have formed a beautiful relationship with her inner Self, becoming an exalted version of the original.

All of the ceremonies will not apply to you, depending upon your age and situation at the time you acquire this book. Additionally, you may not encounter every circumstance that I have created a ceremony for. Every woman does not become a bride, have children, or get divorced. Certain ceremonies may be more appropriately used by your daughters, relatives, or friends, now or in the future. You may find that some of the rituals will have significance later on, as your life changes and you mature. My purpose here was to create a nurturing companion for women that would cover a wide variety of situations and events that we might encounter during our lifetimes.

However, I would encourage you to read all the rituals because you will find it a refreshing experience that will enable you to reassess where you have journeyed from and project ahead to where you eventually will be.

I have divided the ceremonies into broad categories. When closure, for instance, is needed in a woman's life, she can turn to that section to determine what ceremony is appropriate for her particular circumstance. There is a section on birthdays also, which includes a basic ceremony in recognition of this event and several for special birthdays. The beginnings category has ceremonies relating to marriage and children. Wherever you are on your path, there are many ceremonies created for your upliftment, celebration, and healing.

Each chapter has been created to stand on its own. You will find complete details for the performance of every ceremony contained within each chapter. Most of the ceremonies have affirmations that can be used for continuing the momentum gained in the ceremony. All of the ceremonies include journaling exercises.

I believe in freedom of choice. Who am I to dictate to another that my way is the only way? Therefore, every ceremony allows for personal choices to be made. If there is something mentioned that is unappealing in phrasing or motion, for instance, change it. All the rituals have room for individual creativity. Some ask for the composing of a personal prayer. It doesn't have to be fancy or a prize-winner—just let it come from the heart. Even if you have never written anything creative before, let intuition guide you through a new experience.

Throughout the ceremonies I have purposely used a variety of words when referring to a Higher Spiritual Being—called God by some. My intention is to offend no one and include all. If you do not like my selection, insert your own. Whatever you are comfortable with is correct.

It is important to read a ceremony completely before performing it. Tools are needed for all the rituals and special items are requested for some. When reading the ceremony, you may find an area that you want to personalize with your own creativity. Timing and being in the right frame of mind are other essential considerations with some of the emotional cleansing rituals. So please, read each ceremony first before attempting the performance.

Tools for Ceremonies

In any religious ceremony or celebratory act, the use of tools is common. Whenever we attend church, for instance, we can usually expect to see candles burning or hear music in some form being played, whether it is an organ, bells, or voices raised in song. At Fourth of July celebrations, it is common for firecrackers to be discharged and fireworks to be ignited. In military funerals, it is normal to experience guns being fired or even cannons. Candles, music, fireworks, and cannons are all examples of tools that are utilized to raise the energy or vibration during a celebration.

We work with different energy levels, such as sound and aroma, when performing a ceremony, and we employ natural elements to affect a vibration. When we perform a ritual we are in motion, creating a positive movement of energy through a physical demonstration. Ceremony also has the psychological effect of making us feel better. The ceremonial acts in this book are designed to empower women, raise their self-esteem, bring a positive focus into their lives, elevate their spirituality and, therefore, create a more fulfilled existence.

What tools are used depends on what it is that you wish to accomplish. Are you seeking to bring closure to a situation, open yourself to new beginnings, or celebrate change? Everything you will need is listed here and can easily be purchased in bookstores, discount department stores, or New Age shops.

Altar

When you perform these ceremonies, it will be necessary to use an altar. This is a special table designated to hold only your ceremonial tools and should be considered sacred, personal space. Some of the objects that will be mentioned, such as salt, water, and bells, will remain on the altar in between ceremonies.

It is undesirable for other people to handle your tools. These items are sacred to you, and another person's personal energy should not be placed on them by touch. Therefore, it is necessary that the altar be located in a quiet room away from the traffic of people, most preferably in an area that is exclusively your space. If you are a person who meditates regularly, the ideal place would be in the room where you seek the silence. However, if the only appropriate area for meditation and your altar placement is in the bedroom you share with your spouse, lover, etc., that's okay. (Of course, they would have to be open to the idea of an altar in their bedroom.) One would have to assume that in a loving relationship, there would not be a problem with the other person's personal energy being around your tools. However, they still shouldn't be handling them.

If it is not possible to have a private arrangement, a particular table within your home may be designated for this purpose. Your tools would, in that situation, be kept in a special drawer or box, then brought out when needed. I would also suggest that you purify the energy of the table by fanning smoke from smudge or sandalwood incense onto it prior to beginning every ceremony. This will eliminate other people's personal energy that has been left behind when their belongings are placed on the table.

Most people use an altar cloth to cover the surface before placing tools on the table. The cloth should be a natural fabric, such as cotton or silk. White is normally the color used, but if pink happens to be your signature color there is no reason why you can't use it. Some women enjoy selecting different-colored cloths for certain ceremonies. For instance, if you were performing the fiftieth birthday ceremony, you could use a purple cloth for added spirituality. (Refer to the colors listed under the Candles section in this chapter for the meaning of the different colors.) The altar cloth can be plain, fancy, or lacy—the choice is yours. My current selection is a soft green color, which happens to match the walls in my meditation room, and has pink roses embroidered at the corners. Since this cloth is old, and I am an admirer of antiquity, it suits my purposes well.

Water

This wonderful element represents emotional and spiritual energy—no wonder spiritual centers are usually located near it. Water lends cleansing properties to a ceremony. It is fluid, ever in motion, changing form continuously. It is believed to attract spirit energy and is a useful vehicle for all ceremonies. Some people enjoy using water-filled colored glasses during rituals. I personally recommend placing water in a crystal or silver container. It is appropriate to have water present during all the ceremonies and it may remain on the altar afterward, if you choose.

Salt

This is a natural element that some people add to their bath water to purify their aura. Sea salt without iodine is the preferred version because it is the most natural, purest form of salt. Place a small dish of salt on your altar during all ceremonies because it is from the Earth, has grounding benefits, and is a symbol of Earth's wisdom and purity. It is always desirable to bring in the natural elements when performing any ceremony, as you would also be doing when including water or burning incense. Salt may remain on the altar continuously.

Bells

It is a belief in some cultures that the sound of light, sparkling bells ringing will attract friendly spirits. For this reason, it is common to use a tinkling bell during ceremonies. If you want to purify your living quarters, ringing a very loud, heavy bell will eliminate unwanted energy from within the home that may have been left behind due to illness or disposition. By following this act with the ringing of a pretty bell sound, it is believed that you will invite into your dwelling loving spiritual energy.

Those who meditate daily and have an established altar may want to place a crystal or silver bell on their altar to ring when beginning and ending meditations. Also, if it is your desire to attract friendly spirits into your home, hanging wind chimes outside the house is an excellent method.

Sacred Object

During certain ceremonies it is desirable to use an object that you personally feel is representative of something holy or divine, such as prayer beads, a cross, the Star of David, or a statue of Buddha. You may wish to have more than one sacred article, using different tools for various ceremonies. The item(s) can be worn or held and should remain on the altar, unless you do not feel comfortable with a sacred object. If a particular ceremony does not mention a sacred object, but you feel the need, by all means include it.

Drums

Drums are used frequently in Native American ceremonies. It is felt that by beating the drum, songs and chants delivered during ceremonies will be given more intensity because the vibration is being raised through the use of sound. Although I do not specify using drums during any declarations in the ceremonies, if it is your desire to use a drum this would be a good way to provide additional emphasis to your words.

Clothing

When performing ceremonies, wear a special outfit that is used only for these occasions. I wear a long, purple house-dress. I would recommend a garment that is very full and loose, with or without sleeves, that anyone can inexpensively purchase in the lingerie department of any discount store. Other outfits can be worn but whatever you choose, it should be a natural fabric, like cotton or silk, and be loose-fitting. Purple, white, pink, and soft blue are the appropriate colors. I do suggest specific colors in the ceremonies, but if you do not have that particular shade, wear white.

Candle Snuffer

There is a belief that candles do not like to be spit upon when you blow them out. Therefore, it is a nice idea to have a candle snuffer placed on the altar to extinguish the candles. This is an item that should remain on the altar for convenience.

Preparing Yourself

When performing any ceremony, do so with a clean body and clear head. In other words, take a bath or shower and be sober. The very act of cleansing the body is a purification process. We are washing away any barriers so that we will be a clear channel for spiritual energy. Use scented soap, gel, or bath oil to place you in a relaxed state of being through the power of aroma. Sea salt may also be added to the bath water for additional purifying benefits if you feel the need.

Sobriety is important. We do not want to contaminate our personal energy field with substances at this time. This is not to say you should never drink—that choice is yours to make. Just avoid alcohol prior to performing a ceremony. A clear mind is a pure channel for spiritual communication.

Incense

Incense is used in every ceremony and is available in countless fragrances. Each ceremony allows you the choice of a scent that you personally find appealing. The following are the benefits of each incense fragrance:

Sandalwood: generic for a ceremony when you do not have the specific incense on hand; also good for healing.

Jasmine: balance, peace, harmony, love, and protection.

Frankincense: blessings, purification, cleansing, and strength.

Rose: love, balance, creativity, healing, happiness, harmony, and peace.

Myrrh: healing, purification, and cleansing.

Patchouli: love, protection, harmony, and peace.

Cedar: cleansing, purification, harmony, and peace.

Lilac: harmony, peace, and creativity.

Lavender: harmony, peace, healing, love, purification, and cleansing.

Musk: strength and love.

Gardenia: love.

Pine: purification, cleansing, and protection.

Vanilla: love.

Candles

Candlelight enlivens and beautifies our surroundings. It also lends a sacredness to any ceremony. If you have ever attended a church service in the evening amid the glow of candlelight, you have experienced that special reverence only candlelight can give. Your choice of color is important. Several colored candles are used in all the ceremonies in this book.

White: purity, spirituality, and cleansing. Can be used with other colored candles in any ceremony to lend additional spirituality.

Pink: love, be it spiritual or romantic; spiritual awakening and healing.

Yellow or gold: intelligence, the mind, inspiration; useful to bring about change.

Orange: puts things in motion—an action color; good for change.

Green: prosperity in all matters; healing, balance, and renewal in all areas where growth is needed.

Blue: inspiration, wisdom, peace, tranquillity, creativity, and harmony within and without.

Indigo: creativity, inspiration, and spiritual wisdom.

Purple: highest spiritual color, protection, inspiration, and spiritual wisdom.

Brown: grounding and balance.

Red: energy, strength, vitality, and passion for life.

Crystals and Stones

Many people wear stones or crystals on a daily basis to increase prosperity, influence their health, and attract loving vibrations. They are also beneficial in ceremony because they intensify the energy. There are many books currently on the market that can give you more information on this subject. Here is a sampling of stones that you may wish to use in ceremony:

Agate: helps to strengthen the positive; good for health.

Amethyst: also has health benefits. Wonderful for creativity, inspiration, spiritual attunement or communication; helps to bring tranquillity.

Aventurine: creativity; strong healing energy for the heart center, and prosperity in all matters.

Bloodstone: protective properties and helpful with blood-related health issues.

Citrine: aids in uplifting the user; helps to clear thinking when emotions are clouding perceptions.

Diamond: protection and opens crown chakra in spiritual work.

Emerald: good for healing, prosperity, and success.

Fluorite: helps to create a brighter outlook and has grounding benefits.

Garnet: aids clairvoyance; imparts cheerfulness, confidence, and helps in reducing depression.

Jasper: healing; believed by the ancients to have magical properties as an amulet against the evil eye.

Jet: relieves depression and helps to eliminate fear.

Lapis: aids in psychic abilities; helps with depression and improvement of health. Since the Ten Commandments were said to be inscribed on this stone, it is believed that the wearer of lapis carries the God presence.

Malachite: lifts a person's spirits and promotes health and happiness.

Moonstone: inspiration, spiritual guidance, prophecy, and the uplifting of emotions.

Opal: prophecy; helps balance chakras.

Pearl: wisdom and love.

Peridot: the stone of seers and astrologers.

Rock Crystal: stone of clairvoyants, mystics, and healers. Enhances intuition, aids in meditation, and contains protective properties. Useful in all ceremonies.

Rose Quartz: a love stone. Useful for self-love and loving others, creativity, soothing emotions, opening the heart chakra, and hastening recovery.

Snow Quartz: encourages hope and confidence; enhances positive thinking.

Sapphire: calming to the nerves.

Tiger Eye: purifies the system and protects.

Tourmaline: relieves nervousness, anxiety and depression; enhances positive outlook; balances.

Turquoise: considered sacred by some Native American tribes; a powerful protector.

Power Boosters

Certain methods can be employed that will carry over the creative energy you started during the ceremony into your daily life, which will help to manifest your desires. These suggestions are beneficial following any ceremony where you want to inspire future events, uplift emotions, instill confidence, build hope, and so on. Additionally, some of the ceremonies will ask that you create a list of desires or goals. The following will better equip you for success.

Affirmations

If you want to give more energy to your birthday wishes, emotional well-being, or career goals, affirmations can attract wonderful outcomes. Affirmations are designed to stir the divine spark that is within all of us so that we may create an outward manifestation of our desires. Whenever I want to bring attention to a particular area of my life, I create affirmation signs with my computer. I choose a colorful background from the Print Shop program, select pretty lettering, and then place the signs in conspicuous places around my house, such as on mirrors and the refrigerator. Wherever I go, there is a reminder stimulating my subconscious mind into manifesting my desire. If you do not have a computer, ask a friend who does to create the signs for you, or write them yourself with colorful crayons.

When composing the affirmations it is important to make the statements positive and phrased as if they have already occurred. For instance, *I do not crave chocolate* uses a negative word (not), is vague as to when this will happen, and reinforces the idea of chocolate in the mind. A better approach would be, *I am now attracted only to healthy food.*

All spiritual teachers who I am familiar with recognize the value of affirmations and agree that it is preferable to precede affirmations with two words, *I am*. The *I am* represents the divine spark of Spirit within. By using these words we propel spiritual energy into our wishes, which then will flow to the universe to be manifested into reality. However, it is not a mandatory requirement that all your affirmations must be preceded with *I am* in order for them to be effective. The idea is to stimulate the subconscious. If you find it difficult to create a particular affirmation with *I am*, simply compose a positive statement phrased in the present. *The Goddess fills my life with love and happiness now. Spirit now unfolds a golden path created especially for me.*

If you want to change jobs, I would suggest using an affirmation such as *I am now employed by the most perfect company for me at this time. I am attracting to me now the perfect job for my highest and best good.* Affirmations can be spoken, chanted, and thought about. You may want to speak aloud the affirmations every time your attention is attracted to the signs. This will additionally place your affirmations into the vibration of sound, adding even more energy to your desires. If you enjoy drumming, I would suggest allotting some time to beat your favorite drum while you chant your affirmations to add intensity to your words through the sound vibration.

Treasure Mapping

What is a treasure map? This is a personalized wish list, complete with pictures, objects, and words that, when you look at it, will inspire your subconscious to manifest into reality all that it contains. I would suggest spending some time in an arts and crafts store prior to any major birthday or life-changing event that you wish to recognize in ceremony. Here you will find the basic tools you will need to create a treasure map to power-boost your desires.

Select an ample-sized sheet of heavy construction paper, paperboard, or whatever else you might already have around the house that you can attach objects to. Background color is optional. Choose some colorful writing markers or crayons and pick up some glue or rubber cement. Now you have the basics to create a treasure map.

The sheet of paper or cardboard is the foundation on which you will attach pictures from magazines of your perfect vehicle, most desirable home, greatest career aspiration, or whatever it is that your heart desires. Objects can be included, such as pieces of fabric representing the material you wish to be sewn into your wedding gown, a spatula to signify the cooking school you wish to establish, or a paintbrush for your creative genius that has yet to be discovered by the art world. Clip out words from newspapers and magazines, like ARTIST, BOOK OF THE YEAR, CEO, DESIGNER, MANUFACTURER, and CHEF, to state your goals.

I usually recommend working on the treasure map during the week leading up to the birthday or event, as you will see when you read certain ceremonies. This way you are building energy for the performance of the ceremony. However, it is also appropriate to begin a treasure map as part of a ceremony, which I suggest in other rituals. After the ceremony, keep adding bits and pieces as new items come to you. Position the treasure map in a very conspicuous place, such as on the refrigerator or near the bathroom mirror, so that it will frequently be in your line of vision. When you have time, study it at intervals during the day. Let the vision sink into your subconscious mind so that you can bring it into reality.

Journaling

I have found that it is very beneficial to express emotions in a journal. Studies conducted at the University of Texas at Austin over the last fifteen years have shown journal writing to be therapeutic. The subjects who participated in the studies experienced an almost immediate improvement to their immune systems and a lowering of their blood pressure, which lasted several months following the experiment.

Since I believe strongly in journaling, I have made it a part of every ceremony. Specific questions are designed to inspire reflection so that you may find clarification in a problem area, personal growth, emotional healing, or empowerment. Additionally, I recommend in certain ceremonies the benefits of continuing the journaling process for a period of time.

Prior to performing the ceremonies, purchase a pretty journal and a special pen. Even if you already have a journal, designate the new one for use with this book only.

Ceremony

Blessing the Home Environment

Your living space is precious and should be filled with love and light. When circumstances arise in your life that change the energy within your home, such as rambunctious children, chaotic events, teething babies, or visits from people displaying negative attitudes, it is a good time to do a little spiritual housekeeping. It is also wise to do this ritual occasionally to maintain a light-filled environment, which will attract more uplifting energies and positive happenings into your home.

According to the natural laws of the universe, like attracts like. Happiness attracts more happiness. Take a smile, for instance. We are compelled to smile back at someone who is smiling at us. A smile is infectious. We just can't resist! Even a stranger on the street displaying their pearly whites will involuntarily force us into a smile. We have all, at one time or another, experienced the opposite scenario, most likely at work. If an employee is a complainer, for instance, the energy shifts down and everyone consciously or unconsciously feels the effect. We may not have much control over the office, but we can strive to create and maintain a radiant energy within our private abode. Therefore, it is desirable to perform blessings for the house occasionally so we may continually attract brighter moments into our lives.

I usually perform this ceremony alone, but you could include another person if you so desire. Read the complete ceremony prior to beginning the performance and observe the required preparation for yourself. Have a clean body—use a nice vanilla body wash or soap prior to the performance of this ceremony. Wear appropriate colors, such as white, blue, or purple, in a natural fabric. The time of day to perform this ceremony is your choice. The tools you need are:

1. A loud bell or drum.
2. Cleansing incense, such as cedar, lavender, myrrh, or frankincense.
3. A white candle for purity and cleansing.
4. Emerald, bloodstone, or quartz crystal worn as jewelry or carried in a pocket.
5. A religious symbol, such as a cross, holy beads, Buddha statue—whatever you resonate to as being sacred.
6. A gentle bell.
7. A journal and a pen.

Assemble tools 5 and 6 on the downstairs level of your home if it is more than one floor, and the objects in numbers 1 through 4 upstairs. If you live in an apartment, assemble items 5 and 6 at your exit/entrance and tools 1 through 4 at the farthest location from your door. If you have a one-level house with no basement, assemble items 5 and 6 at your back door and tools 1 through 4 at your front door.

Center yourself in the room where you have placed tools 1 through 4. Sit in a comfortable chair or on the floor. Play soft music while you meditate for several minutes, breathing deeply, with your eyes closed. When you feel calm, visualize yourself surrounded by a brilliant white light. See this white light energy reaching outward three feet from your physical form—in front, in back, to each side, above and below. Try to feel the light energy all around you. This is God's white light of love and protection. If it makes you feel more comfortable, you may replace the word God with Goddess, Spirit, Infinite Intelligence, Spiritual Creator, the Force—whatever word that represents the highest spiritual energy to you. Once you feel you have centered yourself, begin the ceremony.

Bless your house with love and light

Either wear the stones or carry them in a pocket. Ring the loud bell or beat the drum throughout your home, making as much noise as possible. I have a large, noisy bell that I use only for this occasion. I would suggest that if you live in an apartment building, you choose a time when few people are home so as not to disturb anyone.

Circle each room while you clang the bell or beat the drum. Continue in this manner until all the rooms have been visited, working your way downstairs (if appropriate), toward the back door, your only exit, or the basement. Be mindful that your purpose now is to create an environment of neutrality. Later you will go back and bless the house with love and light.

Return to your starting place. Hold the candle in one hand and the incense in the other. Allow the incense to enfold you within its smoky aura. Smudge may be used instead of incense, if you choose. The incense will raise the vibrations. The candle symbolically lights your path and adds sacredness to the ceremony. Always be mindful of your candle flame if you are near fabric, and be sure to use a candleholder so no wax drips on your carpet. As you again visit all the rooms, swirl the incense or smudge in a circular manner or figure eight into each of the corners and the center of the rooms. If you have a Christian background, you may wish to form the sign of the cross with the incense or smudge. In each room, recite over and over your specially created declaration, or use my suggestion:

> **The highest and best energy fills my home. God's white light radiates in every room. All the spaces in my dwelling are blessed with white light energy.**

Once you have accomplished this throughout the entire house, you are ready to give an invitation and final blessing. Begin where you have just ended—the back door, exit, or basement. In one hand hold the small bell and in the other the item that represents sacredness to you. Work your way upstairs now, or reverse your previous steps (whichever is appropriate), ringing the bell gently as you circle through each room. Recite a blessing you have created or use my suggestion below. The words do not have to be consistent in each room. If you are gifted with the ability to create lyrical phrases, open yourself up to receive from your intuitive side and recite whatever comes to you. Just keep to the idea that you are blessing the dwelling and welcoming in higher energies, angels, spirits, guardians, etc.

> **This home is blessed with the white light of God. The higher spiritual energies are welcome to share our home, bringing with them health, hope, healing, happiness, and humor. May those from the unseen side of life be loving guardians of our dwelling and bestow upon this home continued blessings for all who abide within.**

Now complete the journaling portion.

Journal Entries

The positive attributes of my home are:

Which room do I feel most comfortable in?

Why am I comfortable in that room?

What would I change in my home?

How can I bring that into reality?

What needs to be eliminated?

How can I make that happen?

What other joys can I add to make this a better environment?

You have just completed spiritual housekeeping!

Affirmations for the Home

I am happy within my home and I love everyone in it

Only peace and goodness dwell within my home

I am re-energized with the power of love
every time I walk into my home

My home is overflowing with love

My home is filled with God's protective white light

Ceremonies for Young Women

Puberty

We can all vividly remember growing through the puberty years: hormones raging, attitudes flourishing, and emotions overflowing. It would have been impossible to foresee all the magnificent opportunities and special blessings that awaited us. Standing at the doorway to womanhood, we could not have been expected at that tender age to understand what it means to be a woman.

Many of us have daughters, granddaughters, relatives, and young friends who will journey on this path. Through them we have the opportunity to contribute to another female's development, leaning on our own wisdom, having been down that road before. By assisting with their transition, we potentially can ease the crossing from childhood into the mysterious realms of womanhood. Through the performance of ceremony, our relatives and friends can become more aware of their feminine energy and begin to understand their own personal power. You, the mother, aunt, grandmother, or friend of a pubescent girl, will facilitate the process of the puberty ceremony.

I would suggest performing the ceremony for puberty seven days after the girl in question has completed her first menstrual cycle. By that time, any discomfort or confusion will not be so prominent in her thoughts. She will be more receptive to the positive side of this life-changing event and more likely to absorb the full benefits of the ceremony. Seven days is significant also because the number seven is a spiritual number, representing mystery, healing, and dreams coming true. If the young relative or friend in your life has already begun menstruating, it is perfectly all right to perform the ceremony now.

It is important to stress the necessity that the girl have a desire to participate in this special ceremony. This is not something that should ever be forced upon her. My friend Mary wanted her daughter, Karen, to perform the ceremony. However, Karen thought her mother had gone bonkers, as she phrased it, for suggesting such a thing. If a situation like this should arise, don't push. Let it be understood that it is her decision. After all, this is her puberty, she should decide whether or not she wishes to perform a ceremony in recognition of the event. If she decides to forgo this acknowledgment, the ceremony can always be done at a later time.

In the case of Mary's daughter, about four months passed following the suggestion of the puberty ceremony when, suddenly, Karen became interested in participating. Mary eagerly arranged everything with great care for the performance of the ceremony. Afterward, she presented Karen with a beautiful basket containing incense, candles, crystals and a copy of this ceremony. As a result of the ceremony, Karen's self-esteem climbed higher and she took more pride in her appearance, much to Mary's delight.

During most of the ritual you will be present, assisting with the assembling of the tools and guiding the procedure. Both of you should read the entire ceremony prior to the performance to be totally prepared.

The necessary tools are as follows:

1. Select an incense that reflects love, balance, and peace, like jasmine or rose.
2. Suggested candles are white for purity; pink, representing love; green for health and balance; and blue for tranquillity and inspiration.
3. Amethyst, bloodstone, moonstone, tourmaline, and especially rose quartz. Use all the stones or as many as you have in your possession. Wear them or place them on the altar.
4. A dish of water.
5. A dish of salt.
6. A silver or crystal bell.
7. A sacred symbol or an object that holds special meaning to the girl, placed on the altar (optional).
8. A journal and a pen.

The facilitator should bathe first, using vanilla or rose-fragranced soap, bath oil or gel, and wear clothing in a natural fabric that is either white or pink. The girl will then begin her part in the ceremony by taking a bath with two tablespoons of sea salt added to bath water scented with either vanilla or rose fragrance. If it is not possible to bathe, then select a shower gel scented with vanilla or rose. A pitcher of water with one tablespoon of sea salt added can be poured over the body while rinsing. Soft music playing would be appropriate and a pink candle burning would be a nice touch also. This should be a relaxing experience and can last as long as the girl desires. After the cleansing, she should slip into some loose clothing in a natural fabric, perhaps even a nightgown. Appropriate colors to use would be white or pink. A floral pattern with these colors is another option.

While the girl is preparing herself, assemble the tools either on your altar, if this feels comfortable to you, or select an appropriate table. You will have to be the judge of where to perform the ceremony. For instance, if this ritual is for your niece, you may be within her home leading the activity. In that case, you will have to select a table from her house and bring the tools with you at a convenient time when no one will disturb either of you. Be sure to cleanse the table with smudge or incense prior to using it.

As you begin the ceremony, play more soft music, light the incense and candles, and have the girl wear and/or hold the stones in her hands. While she is standing in front of the altar, cleanse her with the incense by taking it in your hand and making swirling figure eights or the sign of the cross as you walk around her. Ring the bell three times and ask that the loving female energies of the girl's departed family members attend the ceremony, as is suggested below:

> **I call to all the female spirits in (name)'s family and bid them welcome to this ceremony. Please send your spiritual love to this child who stands at the threshold of womanhood.**

Call them by name, such as, "Grandmother Alice, you are welcome. Aunt Betty, please attend."

Sit together in front of the altar, either on chairs or the floor. Have the girl close her eyes for the meditation. You will guide her, beginning by instructing the girl to take three deep breaths. Read the following aloud, slowly:

> **Bring your attention to the center of your chest. Be conscious of your breathing, in and out, in and out. Feel a relaxing energy settle all around you, calming any anxieties or tension. With every breath you exhale, release these distractions. Feel the spiritual energy that is all about you now. Visualize a beautiful, radiant white light surrounding your physical form. This is a spiritual light, a healing energy that is filled with love. You, (name), are so very loved by all your family members, those who are on Earth and those who dwell in spirit. Everyone wants only happiness, health, and wholeness for you. You deserve**

nothing but the very best in life. As you travel the road to womanhood, along the way you will encounter conflicting emotions, dramatic challenges, and fierce urgings from your body. At these times, know that the situations that present themselves to you are there for your highest growth. They are but stepping stones along your path to maturity. Throughout all of your life, you will grow from your experiences, as you will especially during this pubescent time. Realize that what appears to be important in one moment will cease to be in the next. Take care not to react too hastily in the first moment or you will miss the lesson to be learned. Always hold tight to your true Self, what you know to be right within your heart. Listen to your heart. It will speak to you in the most truthful language of all. When times come that are confusing, know that you may seek the comfort, love, and companionship of me. I will be there for you, always and in all ways.

Slowly take two deep breaths. Gently open your eyes, take another deep breath, and read this prayer.

The girl reads aloud:

Heavenly angels, divine spirits, and ancestral guardians, please guide me as I step upon my pathway to womanhood. Make my journey a safe passage, filled with many happy memories and few bumps in the road. Always let me be aware that I have choices in all situations and that consequences will follow my actions. Guide me to make the appropriate decisions from my heart center so my consequences will be beautiful ones. Teach me to trust my true Self. Help me to stand tall in the face of challenge, always strong in my inner knowledge of right.

> **My body is beautiful. I am a child of God. I am a physical manifestation of the Divine. Spirit lives within this physical shell. My body is the temple of God. For all these reasons, I am capable of many magnificent things. I am a creative, spiritual being. From within me, one day, I have the potential to create new life, another child of God. I will always respect my body in this matter. I have been given a wonderful blessing of life, and knowing this, I will strive to rise to my full potential and bring honor to my Self. I respect the feminine energy that lives inside me and will engage that power when I need strength to meet a challenge. I will always stand ready to be of service to another who is walking their personal path and needs my strength and wisdom. For all my family, friends, and spiritual guardians, I am forever grateful. I pledge to make my Self and you proud. Amen.**

Have her ring the bell three times to conclude the ceremony. Present this budding woman with a special gift that you feel will be appropriate for her. My suggestions would be: a copy of this book, a journal, a silver bell, colored candles, incense, or all of the above! Whatever you decide, be sure to include a journal so that she may continue the process she has started. Explain to her the value of journaling and how it will help her to release those teenage frustrations through the written word. If you have given her this book, she may begin her journaling using the questions that follow. Otherwise, let her copy the questions from your book onto a sheet of paper or into her own journal.

Journal Entries

I am God's most glorious creation because . . .

Creativity manifests itself in my life in what way?

In what areas should I seek to improve myself?

What are the most important things in my life?

Who are the most important people in my life?

Why is this so?

What do I want to be when I grow up?

You are on the road to womanhood now!

Affirmations for Young Women

I am beautiful

I am wise, healthy, and whole

I am a genius at work

Each day brings glorious new experiences

Goddess blesses my every endeavor

I am one with people, animals, nature, and the universe

I am a true and faithful friend

I possess a positive attitude

I reflect God's love on everyone

I am the physical manifestation of the divine

Womanhood

Teenage girls thrive on growing older, unlike most of their mothers. They excitedly anticipate the much-heralded sixteenth and eighteenth birthdays. These two birthdays are joyous episodes in the life of any young female, true landmarks announcing her first steps into adulthood that should be recorded for future reminiscing. This is an excellent time for a special acknowledgment of the passage into womanhood, a private celebration to proclaim to the personal Self that she has hit a milestone, a marker on the road of life. This ceremony may be performed on either the sixteenth or eighteenth birthday, both occasions, or at any time during either particular birth year. The choice is the teenager's to make.

My cousin had been experiencing a strained relationship with her daughter for some time prior to her eighteenth birthday. Sandra felt that Jennifer had a problem being practical, preferring to dream about what she wanted rather than actively participating in bringing things into reality. When Jennifer performed the ritual, she found that the journal exercise provided a way for her to focus on the future. Within a couple of weeks following the ceremony, she decided to attend a local college rather than an out-of-state university and had selected her major. Sandra was thrilled that Jennifer was showing some signs of maturity at last.

Prior to the performance, the young woman and you should read the entire ceremony so that you both are thoroughly familiar with it. Although she will perform this ritual alone, it will be necessary for you to be willing to assist in any way.

It cannot be overemphasized that when performing any ceremony, do so with a clean body and clear head. In other words, the participant should take a bath or shower and be sober. The very act of cleansing the body is a purification process. We are washing away any barriers so that we will be a clear channel for spiritual energy. Use scented soap, gel, or bath oil. A rose or vanilla fragrance is perfect. Two tablespoons of sea salt may also be added to the bath water for additional purifying benefits. Soft music is quieting and a pink candle adds sacredness.

After the cleansing, the young woman should clothe herself in a natural, loose fabric, like cotton. Appropriate colors are white or light blue.

The items necessary to create this ritual are as follows:

1. An incense for creativity, happiness, and balance, like rose.
2. Select all of the following candles: a green candle for prosperity and balance; blue for creativity; brown for grounding; pink for love; and yellow for the intellect and change.
3. The stones best suited are amethyst, aventurine, citrine, fluorite, malachite, pearl, rock crystal, rose quartz, and snow quartz. Use all the stones or as many as you have in your possession. Wear them or place them on the altar.

4. A small bell.
5. A dish of water.
6. A dish of salt.
7. A journal and a pen.

My golden path stretches before me

Play soft meditation music, light all the candles and incense, and sit in a chair or on the floor facing the altar. Ring the bell to signify the beginning of the ceremony. Tilt your head to the right, the left, forward, and then backward. Raise your shoulders up to the ears and let them drop heavily back. Do it once more. Now close the eyes and take several very deep breaths. As you breathe in, feel as if you are breathing in positive, cleansing energy that will help to create positive vibrations in your life. When you exhale, know that you are expelling any impurities that have entered your body, such as germs and pollutants. Breathe in positive energy, exhale all the impure. In with the positive, out with the negative thoughts and attitudes. Do this numerous times until you begin to feel relaxed and comfortable within this peaceful state.

Start to count down from ten to one, slowly, spending time in between numbers to think to yourself one word, *relax*, as you exhale. Ten—relax. Repeat the word again, *relax*, and then move on to the next number: nine—relax—relax, and so on. Now read the following prayer aloud:

> **Heavenly Mother, I call upon you and all the Universal Women in spirit to guide me on my path to womanhood. Those who have gone before me have great wisdom to share and I am open to receiving their knowledge now and in the future. I will listen with keen ears to their melodic promptings so I may better my Earth walk by creating a glow of harmony within my being, which will reflect upon my surroundings at home, school, work, and with friends.**
>
> **This is a blessed day, for it marks exciting new beginnings filled with wondrous surprises to come. I am so very grateful for**

all that I have received and all that I will receive as my life progresses. My heart swells with a joy that can only come from the knowledge that I am a very unique and special woman. Spirit did not make a duplicate of me, nor am I a copy of another. I am me. I am one. I am special. I carry this wisdom proudly within my bosom, never to be forgotten, never to be rejected, always to be cherished.

I am a multitalented, uniquely gifted child of God. I have abilities that are yet to be discovered that abide within me, germinating like the seeds of the sunflower until they blossom into sunny beauty. I am blessed with the inspiration of a poet, the creativity of an artist, and the cleverness of my furry friend the fox. Wisdom is handed to me upon my asking. Agility is granted when I call out. Courage is stored in abundant reserve within my being for use when life demands it be brought forth. Honesty is my partner and friend, guiding me down my path. Faith is my constant companion and hope never leaves me as I make my journey on the road of life.

Many unknowns are hidden around the corners of my future, but I am equal to whatever challenges are placed upon my path. I am comforted in the knowledge that I do not walk this journey alone. The Universal Goddess steers my course around the boulders and pebbles alike. I witness their existence and learn from their appearance so I may avoid repeated encounters. During times of stress and confusion, I know I can count on the Goddess to shelter me, advise me, and love me unceasingly. I am not alone.

I believe that God has a plan for me, a special purpose for my existence. I throw my arms wide to accept my mission and pledge to do my part to create its manifestation. I will not allow

another to detour me from my direction through the issuing of demands that are not for my highest spiritual good. Nor will I be deceived by lofty promises that resonate within me to be false. When doubts rise up in my mind and my heart weighs heavy with confusion, I know the Heavenly Mother watches over me and is only a breath away. I need only seek my personal silence to hear her sweet tones of spiritual guidance.

From this day forward, I walk with the wisdom of the ancients coursing through my veins as I glide through this golden portal into the mysterious realm of womanhood. This is a glorious happening, for today I am an awakened woman!

Ring the bell three times to conclude the ceremony. Now is the perfect time to do some journaling.

Write down all your thoughts and emotions stemming from this ceremony.

Journal Entries

My fondest dream would be . . .

To bring this into fruition I could . . .

What I need to work on most to improve myself is . . .

I am grateful for . . .

I am a multitalented, uniquely gifted child of God in the following ways:

I am a beautiful person because . . .

Go about the business of being a true woman!

The practical answers to my problems are . . .

When in doubt I can always turn to . . .

I have inner strength because . . .

When you are finished, extinguish the candles and apply yourself to living in a manner that will exemplify Perfect Self.

Affirmations for Womanhood

My future is as bright as the sun's rays

The Heavenly Mother brings me only positive thoughts

My highest and best good awaits me now

Protected by Spirit

Spirit watches over my every movement

The Goddess blesses me each morning
through the kiss of the sun

I am God's special child

I am on my path to success

I am beautiful

My golden path stretches before me

Graduation

Graduation from high school or college is one of the most momentous occasions in any person's life. It represents maturity and beginnings. The adult world is waiting with open arms to accept our arrival, the future is pregnant with possibilities, and we are eager to jump headfirst into life! Since graduation marks a beginning brimming with promise for future success, it is a wonderful time to set into motion all sorts of positive energies through ceremony and focus on what is important to you. If you are looking at graduation from the sunny side of thirty, forty, or fifty, for instance, as many women are currently, you will find this cere-

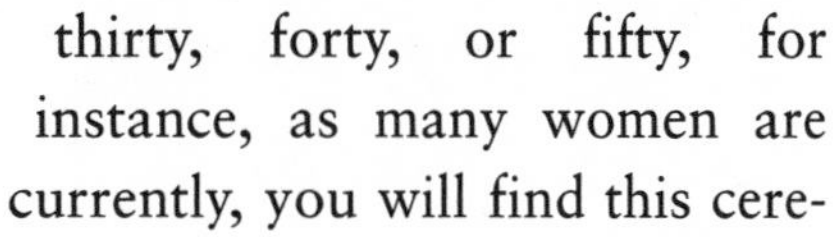

mony equally beneficial. After all, graduation represents bright, new beginnings and a fulfillment of dreams at any age.

During the time Tamara was graduating from college, she was in a state of confusion. She had been offered a position with a prestigious company out of state that was well-suited to her career goals. But her boyfriend, Rick, wanted Tamara to search out a local company so they would not be separated by four states. While Tamara cared for Rick a great deal, she also had visions of grander career opportunities than the area they lived in could provide. Rick began pressing Tamara to marry him, promising he would buy her a little house in a few years, after he had saved enough for a down payment. Tamara wanted to get married—some day. But she felt she was too young, at twenty-two, to leap into such a commitment without first pursuing a career. She was also looking forward to living on her own in a new city and learning to be totally responsible for herself.

Tamara performed the graduation ceremony, hoping it would help her to sort out her feelings. Within a few days following the ritual, she came to realize that Rick was a part of her old life. He was not a motivated career person and did not understand her ambitions. Tamara felt Rick would be better off with another woman as his wife, and left six weeks later to manifest her dreams.

This ritual can be performed any day and time during the week following your graduation. The ceremony should be read in its entirety in advance and all required preparations need to be observed.

It is preferable when performing any ceremony to do so with a clean body and clear head. In other words, take a bath or shower and be sober. The very act of cleansing the body is a purification process. We are washing away any barriers so that we will be a clear channel for spiritual energy. Use scented soap, gel, or bath oil to place yourself in a relaxed state of being through the power of aroma—vanilla or rose are always good choices. Two tablespoons of sea salt may also be added to the bath water for additional purifying benefits. Soft music playing during the bathing period is suggested, and candlelight is always soothing.

After cleansing, clothe yourself in a natural, loose fabric, like cotton or silk. Appropriate colors are white or pink.

Listed are all the necessary tools for the performance of this graduation ceremony:

1. Sandalwood incense.
2. A yellow or gold candle for bringing about change; green for prosperity and balance; and red for strength and passion for life.
3. The following stones: aventurine, emerald, malachite, rock crystal, snow quartz, and tourmaline. Use all the stones or as many as you have in your possession. Wear them or place them on the altar.
4. A small bell.
5. A dish of water.
6. A dish of salt.
7. A journal and a pen.

Play soft music. Begin the ceremony by lighting all the candles and incense and ringing the bell gently, then sitting on the floor or in a chair facing the altar. Close your eyes and shrug your shoulders high up, toward your ears, then release quickly. Do this three times. Bend your head forward, slowly, then backward. Allow the head to drop to the right, then come to the center, and then drop to the left. Bring the head to an upright position. Tense all the muscles in your body, starting at the top with the arms, then release. Continue down until you have tensed and released all your muscles. Take several deep breaths, in and out, in and out, paying close attention to this motion. Now breathe normally, continuing to be aware of your breathing pattern for a minute or so, noticing how your chest expands and deflates, relaxing the entire body in this movement.

Visualize a brilliant ball of white light directly in front of you. This light is the brightest, most intense white light you have ever seen, with glorious shafts of radiant light extending outward in all directions. Feel the warmth that is emanating toward you. The entire frontal part of your body—the face, chest, tummy, and legs—are bathed in warmth. Bask in the light energy as it permeates every pore of your being. Feel this intense white light as it totally fills you up inside and then warms the back portion of your body. Sit a moment within this radiant sauna. Now open your eyes and read the following declaration:

> **Heavenly Mother, I am so very grateful for this time in my life. My heart is bursting with joyous emotion, sending pulsing ripples of rapture throughout my being. I am blessed and privileged to have graduated and I will do my part to bring continued successes into my life. I am proud of me. I have done well. And I will do better. This day is a beginning, a new road opening to lead me on to greater achievements. I am ever so thankful for all those who have helped me become the person I am and who have shared their time and talents with me to make this day possible. I speak their names now aloud.** (Name those who helped along the way by saying, "**Thank you, Grandma,**" etc.)
>
> **I follow spiritually in the footsteps of many who have created great works and know they will assist me from the spirit side of life on my new journey. I need only to call on them to receive their unlimited wisdom and loving guidance. We walk in harmony, partners on a journey focused on success. My highest good is forever protected and guided by those in spirit.**
>
> **My dreams are many, my anticipation great. I am capable of all that I wish to achieve. On this day I pledge to fulfill all my expectations. I will list them now.**

List in your journal everything you wish to personally accomplish. Since this list is intended for only your personal accomplishments, not those involving another, do not include romantic aspirations. Be sure to date your entry so you can look back at this list in the years to come.

Journal Entries

What career do I see for myself?

What talents will I develop further?

Name specific recognition or awards that you seek.

How do I want to be remembered?

How will I make a difference?

Close your eyes and visualize yourself accomplishing your desires. See yourself going through all the motions of creating a great work of art, establishing a successful business, discovering a miracle cure, or whatever it is that you feel will bring you personal satisfaction. See yourself in the future receiving recognition for your achievements. Visualize all this in the most positive, happy manner possible. Everything is wonderful, cheerful, and special. When you are done, recite the following prayer aloud:

> **Thank you, Goddess, for the manifestation of these achievements now. I will do my part to bring about my personal successes by accepting responsibility for all my actions. I will not blame others for my mistakes or procrastination, should I commit those human deeds. I alone am responsible for my outcomes. God helps those who help themselves. With perseverance and angels at my side, I know I can do anything I set my mind to. I am a unique woman; no one else is quite like me. I have**

wonderful gifts to share with the world and it is with pleasure that I set upon my duty to fulfill my promise. I am beautiful. I am talent-filled. I am successful. I am an achiever. I am a child of God. Thank you, Goddess, for my dreams coming true. Amen.

Extinguish the yellow (or gold) candle, saying:

Thank you, Spirit, for the intellect I possess to create my dreams now.

Extinguish the green candle, saying:

Thank you, God, for all the great gifts I am receiving now.

Extinguish the red candle, saying:

Thank you, Goddess, for supplying the vibrant energy to attract my great success.

Ring the bell three times to conclude the ceremony.
Place pen to paper now by journaling your thoughts further.

Journal Entries

What steps must I take to bring my dreams into fruition?

What positive characteristics will enable my success?

Whom do I appreciate most for helping me on my path?

I am grateful for all of these things:

Open your arms to receive!

Affirmations for the Graduate

Goddess walks by my side on this path of life

Spirit guides my every step

I need only ask for God's loving help

I am beautiful and I can do anything

Blessings pour forth from the Goddess' heart

I am whole, healed, and happy

I am talent-filled

I am an achiever

Thank you, God, for my dreams coming true

Thank you, God, for all the great gifts I am receiving now

The Glorious Twenty-First Birthday

I remember how important it was to be twenty-one. This is the height of existence, to be twenty-one: totally, undeniably, a grown-up. Finally matured, an adult, a completely turned-out woman. Yes, that's me, a woman! Embrace this time with open arms and an open mind. The whole world is out there waiting for you to bless it with your talents. You, and only you, can affect the people of the universe with your individual and unique style.

All events in life worth experiencing are certainly due a just acknowledgment. The act of ceremony is quite appropriate at this time to reinforce the magnitude of this birthday. If you participated in any of the prior birthday rituals or the graduation ceremony, then it is likely you will want to perform this very special birthday ceremony also. Or perhaps some wise woman has just given this book to you for your twenty-first birthday!

Being twenty-one held a meaning very dear to Carmen's heart. As a child she had immigrated with her parents from another country where oppression and war were common. The United States of America represented freedom to the family, a privilege that they would never take for granted. Carmen grew up appreciating the benefits she received by living in the United States and looked forward to the day she could vote in elections, viewing this privilege as a sacred trust. Turning twenty-one was truly a glorious day for her.

I am a creative genius

I would suggest performing the ceremony on the morning of this exciting birthday, but if that is impossible, then as soon thereafter as can be arranged during a morning time. Before performing the ceremony, read it in its entirety first.

Prepare for the enjoyment of your birthday. To do this, it will be necessary to arrange ample private time in advance of the big day in which to get reacquainted with your Self. Whatever measures you must go through to allot this time, do it.

Begin your birthday morning by enjoying a gourmet cup of coffee or your favorite tea. While inhaling the aroma of the beverage and becoming aware of your dancing tastebuds, make a list of things you wish to accomplish in the coming year and beyond. Some may be whimsical, others practical, but especially list your heart's desire. If you want to be married and have children, write it down. If you want a career in journalism, write it down. Whatever it is that you feel at this time in your life is what you want for your future, list it.

When writing your wishes, certain phrasing can be beneficial. (Refer to the Affirmations section under The Art of Ceremony on page 15. Your birthday wishes should be written in the same manner.) When you have completed the list, fold the paper in half and then into quarters. Place it on the altar.

Now take that scented, foaming bubble bath you so richly deserve—unless, of course, you don't have a tub. In that case, try a new shower gel in a yummy fragrance, purchased for this special occasion. While you luxuriate in your bath or shower, enjoy the peaceful sounds of soft music. If you are not going into work or to class until much later, if at all (I would encourage the latter), a glass of pink champagne might be in order, or a little champagne mixed with your orange juice. You may also wish to experience all this by candlelight. Do whatever pleases you—this is your day!

The bathing portion of your birthday recognition does not have to be followed by the ceremonial part. You may elect to separate these two segments by going shopping and enjoying a movie after the bath/shower experience, performing the ceremony when you return home. However, if you do follow your bathing with the ceremony, skip the champagne until dinner—you want a clear head for this part. When you decide to perform the ceremony, select a garment of a loose natural fabric, preferably in the shade of soft blue. The tools necessary for the twenty-first birthday ceremony are as follows:

1. An incense for happiness, harmony, love, and peace, such as rose or lavender.
2. The following candles: pink for love; yellow for change; green for prosperity and healing; and blue for peace and creativity.
3. The following stones: agate, amethyst, aventurine, emerald, jet, malachite, rose quartz, and snow quartz. Use all the stones or as many as you have in your possession. Wear them or place them on the altar.
4. A dish of salt.
5. A dish of water.
6. A small bell.
7. A fireproof dish.
8. The list of wishes.
9. A journal and a pen.

Light all the candles and the incense, play soft music, and then ring the bell three times to start the ceremony. Sit comfortably on the floor or in a chair facing the altar. Close your eyes and inhale deeply several times. Visualize a large sun over the top of your head, a bright gleaming orb of brilliant yellow light. Feel the radiance falling down upon the top of your head, the warmth gently touching the crown. Now see the sun as it slowly draws closer, making its descent. When the sun touches the top of your head, it will break open like a cracked egg and the golden, light energy will be released to slide down over your face, the back and sides of your head, down the neck, and over the shoulders. See the light energy as it continues to flow down your torso and feel the warmth as it touches each part of your body. As this sun-energy flows through your legs, feel as if it is washing away any tensions. Sit for as long as you want to contemplate your future. Visualize all the wonderful events in your life that you previously listed on paper that you wish to manifest into reality one day. When you are done, open your eyes and read this declaration:

> **Universal Heart, it is with love that I come to you. For my life I desire many things. Some dreams are for material accomplishments, while others contain the hope for true love. I am young and do not know what Spirit will bring to me during this incarnation on Earth. I trust that whatever I receive will be for my highest and best good. It is with a happy heart that I look to the future, and with wide-flung arms that I stand ready to embrace what is mine to possess. Jealousy is not an emotion I own, because I know no one can take from me what is rightfully mine. Disappointments are merely minor detours along my path to perfection, and I must realize that at these intervals Spirit is at work for my highest and ultimate good. Even when I feel that a particular situation or desire is for my best development, if it does not manifest as I wish, then I must trust that it will be proven in time to be better in another form. I know it is a wise woman who recognizes that her once-chosen desire will be replaced by something greater. Spirit is wiser and I must trust the process as these events challenge my well-being, knowing that the Goddess stands ever-present at my side. I will remember that I am eternally protected as well as directed from the spirit side of life.**

My body is filled with the strength and ability to succeed when I place my focus intensely. I instinctively will know when the challenges presented to me are to be tackled with unrelenting fervor or when it is a sign that something better is coming and I must not continue my pursuit. God has placed within me a confidence that is steady and a sensitivity that is keen. My intuition will serve me well as I trek down my path. Unscathed I will go if I pay attention to my inner voice.

In the silence I will sit to receive the wisdom of Spirit. My Self requires spiritual nourishment and I desire to fulfill all my soul's needs through communion with Spirit. The Goddess will soothe me when I am bruised, encourage me when I am disheartened, guide me when I am confused, and celebrate my happiness when I am joyful. I know through spiritual guidance that I can tap into the seeds of wisdom and cultivate the rose of my dreams, which will bloom into a magnificence that God will admire.

Pick up the folded list of your desires from the altar and touch the paper to the flame of the green candle so it will ignite. Say aloud the following:

May my desires be lifted high on the smoke of this candle so they may be blessed thrice by God, Goddess, and Spirit.

Place the burning paper into the fireproof dish so it may safely turn to ashes. Say the following prayer aloud:

Father, Mother, God, I give heartfelt thanks for the manifestation of these desires.

Extinguish the pink candle, saying:

Goddess loves me and brings only my highest and best good to me.

Extinguish the yellow candle, saying:

I welcome positive change within my life.

Extinguish the green candle, saying:

I am healthy, wealthy, and wise today.

Extinguish the blue candle, saying:

Peace fills my being and creative energy fills my soul.

Take the ashes outside and either bury them or let them float off in the breeze. Speak these words aloud:

Entwine with nature to manifest the fabric of creation.
(Shout: **"Yes!"**)

Return to the altar and ring the bell three times to conclude the ceremony.

It is always appropriate to journal following a birthday ceremony. Please continue.

Journal Entries

In the next five years, I can see myself . . .

It would make me supremely happy to be involved in . . .

I wish to learn to . . .

If there was one thing about myself I would change now, it would be . . .

How can I achieve this?

My strongest talents to promote are . . .

If I do not receive what I desire when I believe it should happen, how will I handle that event?

In what manner can I help others?

Be about the business of your life!

Affirmations for Being Twenty-One

I am receiving my highest and best good now

I am prosperous in all the events of my day

I am a creative genius

Goddess blesses all my opportunities

My every breath draws to me positive happenings

Prosperity is attracted to me now

Love is always the answer

I am healthy, wealthy, and wise

I open my arms wide to receive the bounty
God has prepared for me now

Peace fills my being and creative energy fills my soul

We Celebrate All Birthdays

Recognizing the Birthday

No one quite like you—with your particular talents, captivating charm, and personal aura—has ever been created before, nor will they be again. No regrets are allowed, or bemoaning that you are another year older. A special day was chosen for unique you to be born! The whole of the universe deliberately selected the specific time, day, location, and year. You are special. Every life is precious. Every life is divine. And you are beautiful! How could you not be beautiful when you are a child of God? Infinite Intelligence, Spirit, Goddess, whatever name you choose to call this spiritual energy force, created you. This is a glorious day because it is your birthday—you divine creature, you, this is your day. And you are going to celebrate this momentous occasion, the day you were born, like you never have before—through the act of ceremony!

Congratulations are the only order of the day. This is a day worthy of honor, recognition, and celebration. This is the first day of your individual New Year. You are about to embark on another journey on the road of life. You can anticipate a variety of events, everything from lusty happenings to a couple of poop-outs. Life. Did you know that if we didn't have an occasional bump in the road of life, we wouldn't be capable of appreciating or even recognizing all the wondrous happenings in our lives? Life. Be excited about it! The very word itself is positive. Life! Be joyous that you have a life! Let your heart leap with anticipation for all the wonderful adventures that are forthcoming! This is a new year, a new beginning—a fresh start on your path. Cherish this day, for it will bring whatever you project.

Prepare for the enjoyment of your birthday

Prepare for the enjoyment of your birthday. To do this, it will be necessary to arrange ample private time in which to get reacquainted with your Self. Whatever measures you must go through to allot this time, do it. It may be hard to believe, but it is permissible to come into work late one day a year or even take the day off! You will thank yourself for allotting this precious private time. Please read the entire ceremony first.

Begin your birthday morning by languishing over a gourmet cup of coffee or your favorite tea. While inhaling the aroma of the beverage and becoming aware of your dancing tastebuds, make a list of things you wish to accomplish in the coming year. Most should be practical, while others need to focus on fun. When writing your wishes, certain phrasing can be beneficial. (Refer to the Affirmations section under The Art of Ceremony on page 15. Your birthday wishes should be written in the same manner.)

As a counselor, I have found it is common for women (and men) to fly around in six directions. By this, I mean that sometimes people have so much energy, they want to be involved in everything. They join clubs, become active in churches, and participate in social issues to the point of being fragmented. Katherine is a perfect example of this behavior. She always said yes to requests to do tasks within the organizations of which she was a member. While this was a noble deed, she never stopped to consider that she also worked full time, had a family, and was already deeply involved in numerous church activities. Consequently, other volunteers became frustrated when Katherine never finished her tasks. The problem with Katherine was that in her heartfelt desire to participate, she was unable to apply herself to the best of her ability in any one area because her energy was divided in too many directions. Thus the term "flying around in six directions."

The purpose for writing down the desires for the coming year is to bring a clear perspective into where we want to journey. Living a balanced life is vital to our spiritual well-being. We must recognize the importance of allotting time for fun, otherwise we become out of balance. All work and no play makes for one dull Jane! Fun enlivens our soul, rejuvenates our spirit, and makes our body sing with vitality. Therefore, it is mandatory to include "fun" in the list!

When you have completed the list, roll it into a cylinder and fasten it with a ribbon or hair tie. Set it on the altar to be used later in your ceremony.

Now take that scented, foaming bubble bath you have deserved for far too long—unless, of course, you don't have a tub. In that case, try a new shower gel in a delicious fragrance, purchased for this special occasion. While you luxuriate in your bath or shower, enjoy the peaceful sounds of soft music. If you are not going into work until much later, if at all (I would encourage the latter), a glass of pink champagne might be in order, or a little champagne mixed with your orange juice. You may also wish to experience all this by candlelight. Do whatever pleases you—this is your day.

The bathing portion of your birthday recognition does not have to be followed by the ceremonial part. You may elect to separate these two segments by going shopping by yourself or with friends and enjoying a movie after the bath/shower experience, performing the ceremony when you return home. However, if you do follow your bathing with the ceremony, skip the champagne until dinner. Whenever you decide to perform the ceremony, wear a comfortable cotton fabric in the shade of pink or white. The tools you will need to perform your birthday ceremony are:

1. Your favorite incense for love, creativity, harmony, and happiness, like jasmine, rose, patchouli, or lilac.
2. Choose a pink candle for love; a green one for balance and growth; and blue for your creativity. You may wish to place a purple candle on the altar to reflect your spiritual side.
3. Amethyst, aventurine, malachite, moonstone, and especially rose quartz. Use all the stones or as many as you have in your possession. Wear them or place them on the altar.
4. A dish of water.
5. A dish of salt.
6. A small bell.
7. A journal and a pen.
8. The rolled cylinder list for the year, placed on the altar.

Light the candles and incense. Sit in a chair or on the floor in front of the altar. The stones on the altar may be held in your hands, if you wish. Ring the bell, then close your eyes and take three long breaths, slowly exhaling each time through your lips. As you exhale the third time, visualize your breath streaming out in front of you, like white smoke. This is the white light of the Goddess within, the Infinite. See the white light energy begin to change form, expanding in all directions to enclose you within its protective, loving embrace. Feel the comfort within your cocoon of light. Enjoy this feeling of unconditional love. You are a child of God. Goddess loves you all ways and always. Allow relaxation to penetrate your being. Feel your body become loose, starting at the top of your head, slowly relaxing all the way down to your feet. Reflect on all your positive attributes, fine qualities, and special talents. Allow those early morning dreams and desires that you placed on your list to float into your consciousness. Play with them. Visualize yourself making your heart's desire manifest. See yourself going through the motions of creating your dream. Take as long as you feel necessary to complete this portion of the ceremony. When you are through, read aloud the following prayer:

Heavenly Mother, I give grateful thanks for this blessing of life. I sit before my altar in recognition of this wondrous day of creation. I am so very happy to be alive, giving honor to my Self on this, my (number) birthday. My heart is full. I can feel it swell with love for me. It overflows with affection and splashes fond blessings all over my soul, spirit, and physical being. I am bathed in love. I am a child of God. I am happy, whole, healed, and filled with the energy of love. My future is bright and growing even more radiant each year. Every birthday marks another year's wisdom gained. My lessons of the past will serve me well in this new birth year.

Allow me to be open to receive messages of guidance, that I may hear clearly my direction from that small voice within. Help me to fulfill my desires of earthly accomplishments. Please lay the signs along my pathway in a manner I may easily interpret. I speak aloud these dreams for my future, placing them into safekeeping with the universe through the vibration of sound, and anticipate an abundant, speedy return. (Read aloud your fondest desires from your list.) **Heavenly Mother, Divine Father, Spirit, I give gracious thanks for these blessings I am receiving now. I thank you for their manifestation. Amen.**

Take the cylinder list and go outside. Bury it in the earth, anticipating your desires will germinate and be blessed by the Mother Earth energy. Say a private prayer. Go back inside and ring the bell on the altar three times to conclude your birthday ceremony.

If it is impossible to bury the list in the earth because you live in an apartment in New York City, for instance, I would suggest leaving the list on the altar so it will receive blessings every time you meditate or perform other ceremonies.

Now, create affirmation signs using as many of your wishes as you want. Place them about the house in all the conspicuous places you frequent. Remember, by reciting them aloud whenever your eyes catch sight of the affirmations, you will be placing additional energy upon your wishes through the vibration of sound.

Creating a treasure map (see page 16) would be additionally beneficial to bring into fruition your desires. Do it now, while the energy is flowing! When it is complete, position the treasure map so you can focus on it every day while you sip your morning coffee, thereby allowing your brain to bring into reality all your hopes and dreams. This can be your most prosperous year ever! Take advantage of all the tools the universe has provided to help you fulfill your dreams.

With so many assignments to complete in the celebration of your birthday, you may choose to perform the following journaling exercise later in the day. Otherwise, continue now to commit your feelings to paper.

Journal Entries

Why is it important in this particular year that I achieve my goals?

Some of the ways I could bring my dreams into reality are . . .

What self-imposed obstacles do I have a tendency to create that would deter my success?

What steps can I take to correct this?

Where is my strength when life throws me the proverbial curve ball?

What steps should I take so I feel more empowered?

When all is said and done, what is truly the most important element in my life?

Smile! Your new life has just begun!

Birthday Affirmations

Angels light my path, making my passage easy

I am filled with the energy of love

The Heavenly Mother guides me at every turn

Success is my companion each day

I am happy, healthy, whole, and healed

I am surrounded by Spirit's light as I chart my course this year

Spirit shines the light of prosperity on all my endeavors

All my paths lead to my highest and best good

I give grateful thanks for these blessings I am receiving now

My future is bright and growing more radiant each year

The Thirtieth Birthday

A common sentiment expressed frequently by women is that they suffered greater anxiety over the approach of their thirtieth birthday than they did of the fortieth. I must confess being among that crowd. I tortured myself all through my twenty-ninth year, feeling old and miserable, dreading the next birthday. By comparison, my fortieth birthday was a piece of cake.

I don't know why we react so strongly to the big 3-0. Maybe it is because throughout our young lives we have always desired to be older—loved it, even greeted each birthday with open arms. Then suddenly the thirty-year mark looms ahead and we become paranoid at the prospect of getting old. Not older, old. At thirty we cannot be considered children or even young adults. We have matured. We are truly adults, complete with major adult financial responsibilities. That translates into being old, becoming just like our parents. To make matters worse, if we have not yet met the infamous Mr. Right, the idea of turning thirty can also signal to our nervous brains that we have become an old maid. Let me hasten to state that no one is an old maid at the age of thirty. Let us finally dispense with that antiquated terminology and remember that we are enlightened, aware women—women who can choose not to be married and still live wonderfully happy existences.

If you are disturbed because your thirtieth birthday is drawing close, please remember that it all depends on which side of thirty you rest on as to how you perceive this event. In retrospect, most older women feel it would be great to be thirty again—so full of health, vitality, and filled with inspiration and energy. Within our being lies experience and some wisdom. Ahead, life offers so many glorious opportunities. Please enjoy this special time in your life, and create wonderful memories during this decade. One day you will look back on this time and laugh at your self-induced paranoia! (Trust me on this one.)

One of the purposes of this book is to encourage women to acquire a positive attitude regarding all situations. This applies equally to those birthdays we do not relish. With the approach of the thirtieth birthday, it is important to ignore what you perceive to be negative about a new decade or what you may fear about the future. Focus instead, intensely, on all the wonderful things you want to accomplish and experience. The week leading up to your thirtieth birthday should be spent in preparation for the big event. If you don't have free time, make room for it. This is important to your well-being. If you can't find time to be good to yourself, what kind of a Self are you going to be to others? What example are you setting for your spouse, children, significant other, siblings? Here's what I want you to do:

One week prior to your birthday, begin to create a treasure map. Page 16 details treasure mapping if you have never done one or a significant amount of time has passed since the creation of the last one. The first step is to give due consideration to your desires for the future, your aspirations. Then, begin to collect items that represent your wishes. Place these significant articles, words, and papers on the treasure map as they come into your hands. By working with the treasure map during the week leading up to your birthday, you will be building energy for the ceremony.

My friend Linda very carefully selected the pieces of her treasure map. Every time she added an additional phrase of inspiration or article to the foundation of the map, she got a little more excited. She viewed each addition as another stepping stone on her path that would lead her closer to her goals. When Linda's birthday arrived, she felt she had created a masterpiece that would stimulate the creation of her dreams. During the course of the year, whenever she questioned her success, Linda would devote time to studying her treasure map. She found that she received renewed faith in the process and gained insight. Did all her dreams manifest? The ones she focused the most energy on did. The ones that did not manifest, interestingly, lost their importance along the way.

A clearer vision is before me now

On the day of your thirtieth birthday, pamper yourself. Begin your birthday morning by leisurely enjoying a gourmet cup of coffee or your favorite tea. While inhaling the aroma of the beverage and becoming aware of your dancing tastebuds, gaze at your treasure map. Allow the images to become attached to your psyche.

Now take that scented, foaming bubble bath you so rightfully deserve—unless, of course, you don't have a tub. In that case, try a new shower gel in a tantalizing fragrance, purchased for this special occasion. While you luxuriate in your bath or shower, enjoy the peaceful sounds of soft music. If you are not going into work until much later, if at all (I would encourage the latter), a glass of pink champagne might be in order, or a little champagne mixed with your orange juice. You may also wish to experience all this by candlelight. Do whatever pleases you—this is your day.

The bathing portion of your birthday recognition does not have to be followed by the ceremonial part. You may elect to separate these two segments by going shopping with friends and enjoying a movie after the bath/shower experience, choosing to perform the ceremony when you return home. However, if you do follow the bathing portion with the ceremony, skip the champagne until dinner. Whenever you choose to perform the ritual, wear a loose-fitting, natural fabric garment in soft blue or white.

Assemble the following items for the ceremony and be sure to place the treasure map you have started near the altar.

1. Rose incense, so full of love, happiness, and creativity.
2. The best candles to choose are pink for love; yellow for the intellect and change; green for prosperity, balance, and renewal; and purple for inspiration and wisdom.
3. Amethyst, aventurine, citrine, diamond, emerald, garnet, malachite, moonstone, pearl, rock crystal, rose quartz, snow quartz, and tourmaline. Use all the stones or as many as you have in your possession. Wear them or place them on the altar.
4. A dish of water.
5. A dish of salt.
6. A small bell.
7. A journal and a pen.

Light all the candles and the incense, have soft music playing, and ring the small bell to start the ceremony. Now sit comfortably in front of the altar, on the floor or in a chair. Take several deep, slow, refreshing breaths of air. Breathe another series of deep, cleansing breaths while visualizing the energy of the air entering your body through the heart center and exiting through the mouth. Continue to visualize the breath as it enters and exits while you now breathe normally. Slow and controlled, easy in, easy out. Feel your body become relaxed as you focus on your breathing pattern for a few minutes. Now become aware of a brilliant white light—so bright, so beautiful—just before you, radiating outward, warming the front of your body. Welcome the white light as it draws closer to your being. Feel your body glow and grow warmer as the light continues to be attracted to you. Allow the white light energy to come closer until it totally surrounds your physical body. Feel the healing warmth of this intense energy force as it permeates deep within your being, touching your soul. Sit for a few moments within the white light of God. Then take three deep breaths to fill your lungs with the white light energy. Read the following declaration aloud:

> **I call to the angelic kingdom, my ancestral mothers in spirit, and my spiritual guardians to attend me now. I request humbly their companionship and blessings on this special day, my birthday. I stand at the threshold of another decade, a new beginning. This decade is like a labyrinth, full of mystery and challenge, compelling me to enter. My being is filled with curiosity and wonder. Excitement flickers in my stomach. What lies ahead? I hear angelic voices sweetly whispering repeatedly one word in my ear. "Trust." "Trust." "Trust." I am comforted.**
>
> **My heart knows that the Goddess stands just around the first corner with her arms spread wide to encircle me within her protective embrace. She is ever present, ever faithful. She knows my needs and will provide for me as she always has before. My successes have been many and will continue to unfold as I happily anticipate everything this new decade holds for me. I am successful. I am accomplished. I am creative. I am on a unique journey, filled with radiant opportunities and vast achievements. Yes! My magnificent being is in a state of metamorphosis, much like the caterpillar that evolves into the glorious butterfly. I feel more electric, more vibrant. My butterfly wings are spreading wide, forming an umbrella under which all goodness and wisdom germinates for me. With an open mind, I accept and welcome change. Standing within the radiant light reflecting from the Goddess, I know that only beauty and bounty await me in this next decade because only love and happiness pave this new road.**

Turn your attention to the treasure map. Pay close attention to what you have thus far included in its contents. As you study the pictures, words, and objects, see yourself being involved in the acts necessary to bring your desires into reality. Take your time. These are your dreams; drink them in. Close your eyes, if you wish, to more fully visualize. When you are done, read aloud the following prayer:

> **The Divine Mother and I are in perfect balance. I feel her presence constantly. She guides my every move, influences my daily thoughts, and lends unending support and loving protection. I know my path through this next decade will be abundant with bountiful rewards. If I doubt, she will encourage. If I become weak, she will strengthen. If I fail, she will show me the wisdom gained. I trust in the knowledge that new opportunities intended for my highest and best development will arise at the appropriate time, as they always have in the past. I put my trust in Spirit's wisdom, knowing it will lead me to grander endeavors than I can imagine at this time.**
>
> **Spiritual Creator, together we will build an emotional structure that will be the foundation upon which I will draw strength. I am blessed to be born at this particular period in time where I can be free to express myself and assist in the spiritual and personal development of others. The more I attune to my inner Self the greater my inspiration and creativity becomes. I am filled to overflowing with divine gifts that I wish to share. I am greatly honored and deeply pleased to assist in the prosperity of others, for this is our personal obligation while on the Earth plane. As I help one, I help all. As I help another, they help me. This is the circle of life. Together we create abundance.**
>
> **Guardians, I know that you cocoon me within the white light of love, protection, healing, and regeneration. My thoughts are**

the positive reflections of the wise women, and therefore I see only the good in every situation. My heart is open to understanding. I do not judge, but rather feel compassion. Joy is present in my stride. I am so very grateful to my ancestral women for blessing me with a courageous heart. I feel the enduring strength of our bond. Together we are an invincible force that is created through love. With all of them standing behind me, I walk forward each day internally powered by love, touching each person in a very special way. Thank you all for your gifts of love. Amen.

When you are done, place your treasure map wherever you have decided it will give you the most benefit. Return to the altar and begin to extinguish the candles.

Snuff out the yellow candle, saying aloud:

I happily welcome change into my life.

Snuff out the green candle, saying aloud:

I am so very grateful for the prosperity and balance in my life.

Snuff out the pink candle, saying aloud:

I give humble thanks for the love I have received from all my spiritual guardians and ancestral women.

Snuff out the purple candle, saying aloud:

I am blessed with the wisdom and inspiration of the Goddess.

Ring the bell three times to conclude the ceremony.

Stretch your body and get something tasty to drink, then complete the journal exercises that follow.

Journal Entries

I am entering the most glorious decade of my life because . . .

I will become prosperous beyond my dreams by applying . . .

My creativity is best demonstrated at this time through . . .

I can strengthen my feelings of self-empowerment by . . .

I used to think ____________ was so important. I now realize it is not. Why?

I am most grateful for . . .

In the next ten years I can see myself . . .

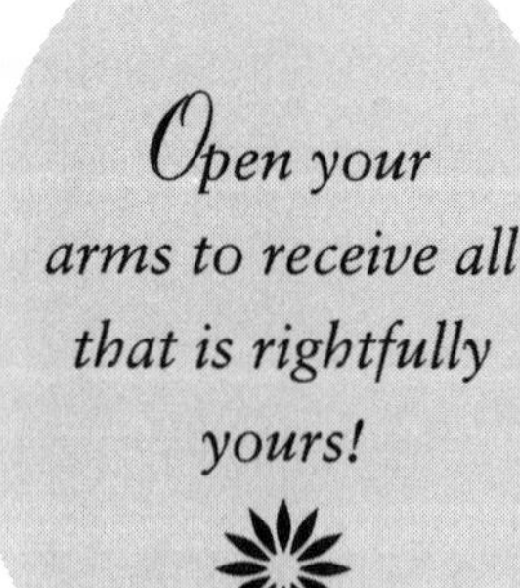

Open your arms to receive all that is rightfully yours!

Thirtieth Birthday Affirmations

Whatever the question, love is the answer

A clearer vision is before me now

I am a creative genius

Goddess fills my heart with love and my head with wisdom

Creative energy surrounds my every endeavor

Prosperity is attracted to me now

The Divine Mother blesses all my endeavors

I am in a sacred bubble filled with Goddess love

God loves me

I am blessed with the wisdom of the Goddess

Turning Forty, Fifty, and . . .

Every time we enter into another decade, we are surrounded by new personal energy. A plethora of possibilities stands before us. However, some women intentionally miss the opportunity to bring recognition to their fortieth and fiftieth birthdays, choosing instead to proclaim themselves thirty-nine forever or forty-five eternally. Let us please choose to pass through this portal into our next decade by glorifying these special birthdays through the performance of ceremony, realizing that a new realm of adventure awaits!

One of the wonderful things about living during this period of time is that there are so many women extolling the joys of being forty, fifty, and beyond. Everywhere we look are examples of women living a large life full of energy, brilliance, and creativity. There are so many ladies presently who are in their fifties—and looking GOOD—we don't even know what fifty looks like anymore!

In a society that seems to worship youthful faces and figures, we have women who epitomize class, wit, intelligence, character, achievement, and sex appeal who would not be considered young on a chronological scale. Tina Turner, with her dazzling legs, is still rocking our souls. Gloria Steinem's inner beauty radiates from her face and demeanor, and her striking intelligence is admirable at any age. Madeleine Albright, as a representative for the United States, is an impassioned negotiator who commands respect all over the world. Eunice Kennedy Shriver, founder of Special Olympics, demonstrates the difference one woman can make. And Lauren Bacall—who wouldn't want to be blessed with her regal qualities? Ladies, we are in good company!

I possess the wisdom of the Goddess

I turned fifty this year, and I did something some people would view as foolish. I got a tattoo—a butterfly—on the inside of my left ankle. You might wonder what would possess me to do something so permanent to my body. Besides that it happens to be a very popular thing to do currently, there was also a personal reason, which I will share.

The idea to get a tattoo was not a spontaneous decision or a case of a woman seeking to regain her youth. I contemplated getting a tattoo for almost two years. I just happened to get really serious about becoming tattooed around my fiftieth birthday. The hardest thing about it was deciding what design would decorate my ankle for the rest of my life. It had to hold meaning so that when I looked at my tattoo, I would feel some sense of inspiration. I spent many hours on the Internet viewing tattoos and visited tattoo parlors. The first place I went to was straight out of a B movie, complete with a Harley Davidson propped up in the entranceway and tattooed biker-type men behind the counter who used colorful language. The manager was polite to me and pleasant enough—he answered all my questions—but I did not feel like I belonged there.

The tattoo parlor I decided on had a very humorous man as the sole proprietor. I felt much more comfortable with him. He also had so many feminine designs to choose from that the decision became easier to make. Also around the time I was seeking my perfect tattoo, I read an article written by a women who, when she turned fifty, got a tattoo. She had wings placed on her inner ankle, which had a personal symbolic meaning to her.

Suddenly it occurred to me that wings held a significance for me also. I loved butterflies. Butterflies are free—that held meaning. Freedom of choice. Freedom to be who I am. My mother thought I should be cast in the same mold as her. Forget about asserting one's own individuality, I was taught to conform. It was more important to be concerned about what the neighbors and everyone else thought rather than being who I was. I was supposed to remain a caterpillar, not evolve into the beautiful butterfly.

I saw the butterfly as a badge of freedom, symbolizing the real me, the me my mother attempted to squash in hopes of cultivating a better model. I knew sporting a tattoo might attract some disapproving looks, but I felt that would even assist in my pursuit not to be so concerned about what other people thought.

I love my tattoo. I think it is sexy. And so far I have only received compliments. I'm not advocating every woman should run out and get a tattoo, but it was right for me because it assisted in my development and empowerment. It helps make me proud to be who I am.

Let us all be proud of who we are, no matter what stage of our path we are presently walking. We are wise, we are strong, and we have gone the distance. The best is yet to come because we have only just begun.

The first ceremony is intended to be used by women who are turning forty. It is a ritual designed to be performed alone. Please read the entire ceremony a few days ahead of time so that you can make appropriate arrangements for your special day. There is a certain amount of planning required, especially if you intend to take the day off from work.

Forty

On this special birthday, sleep in an extra couple of hours—you deserve it. Then begin preparing yourself for the ceremony in a leisurely fashion. As with all birthday mornings, you should spoil yourself unmercifully. Enjoy that gourmet coffee or special tea. Read the newspaper from cover to cover. Indulge in something sinful for breakfast. Hey, it's your birthday!

While inhaling the aroma of the beverage, which should have placed you in a peaceful state of mind, make a list of things you wish to accomplish this year. When you have completed that, write another list projecting for the new decade. Certain phrasing is beneficial—refer to page 15 if you need a refresher on how to do that, under the subheading Affirmations. Roll each list and fasten with a hair ribbon or hair tie when completed.

The tools you will need for this ceremony are as follows:

1. Choose an incense for balance and harmony, like jasmine or rose.
2. Select a green candle for balance and renewal; pink for spiritual awakening and love; blue for inspiration and peace of mind; and purple for spiritual wisdom.
3. Amethyst, diamond, malachite, moonstone, rock crystal, and especially rose quartz. Use all the stones or as many as you have in your possession. Wear them or place them on the altar.
4. A sacred object.
5. A dish of salt.
6. A dish of water.
7. A gentle bell.
8. Birthday lists, tied with a ribbon.
9. A journal and a pen.

Prepare yourself in the normal manner by bathing with aromatic soap, body wash, or gel amidst candlelight and soft music. You may enjoy sipping a glass of pink champagne or another cup of coffee or tea, especially if you are fortunate to be able to soak in a tub. Take time to lavish body lotion all over your body, enjoying the scent and sensation of its coolness.

After you have cleansed yourself, you may either perform the ceremony or perhaps choose to dash off for a shopping spree and a movie, like I normally suggest. Of course, if you elect to perform the ceremony immediately, do not drink the champagne until dinner.

When you do perform the ceremony, dress in a natural fabric in the color of white or purple. Begin by lighting the candles and incense while soft music is playing. Take the incense from the altar and move it in a figure eight fashion as you turn slowly in a circle, so the smoke blends with your aura. Return the incense to the altar and sit on the floor or in a chair in front of the altar. Ring the bell three times.

Take three deep breaths with your eyes closed. Begin to release any tension you may feel. With every exhalation, feel as if any frustrations or concerns are leaving your body and mind. Feel the radiant warmth of a bright, golden light directly over your head. As you visualize the yellow-white rays extending down from this ball of golden light, feel the relaxing energy as it touches the top of your head. Be aware of the warmth and see the brilliance of the light energy as it slowly cascades over your face, shoulders, and back, down your torso and arms into the hip area, sweeping into the thighs and down the legs to the feet. Visualize your entire body surrounded by the golden light. You are cocooned within the light energy of wisdom. Goddess light enfolds you within the center of the all-knowing, all-seeing, all-creative womb. For a moment, allow the highest of spiritual energy to penetrate within. Be open to the images that will dance in your head. When you are ready, take a deep breath, open your eyes, and read the following prayer:

> **Goddess, bless me always and in all ways. Help me to continually see my inner beauty as I evolve into a magnificent, glorious butterfly. I lift my spiritual wings in praise of thee and me as I continue to float through life's experiences with courage in my heart and strength in my step. Please remind me daily how wise I have become through my travels in this lifetime. My wisdom has expanded to such depths that I only need to sit in silence to receive the words of truth. I now trust that small voice within to**

speak to me in ways no earthly creature could. I am in touch with my Self and for this I am eternally grateful.

I give sincere honor and humble recognition to those before me who have set in motion conditions that enable women like myself to follow our hearts' desires and receive our highest good. Let me also be an example to others so they, too, may capture their dream within their butterfly wings and bring it to manifestation.

As I begin my new journey, my next spiritual adventure, keep wide my eyes to view the wondrous happenings that are just ahead. I open my heart to the magnificent bounty that I am to receive each moment in the coming years. I bless every circumstance that is before me because each experience is a new lesson for my spiritual growth. Only good can come to me now as I place my feet upon the path I have spiritually chosen. Each turn will only bring more wisdom, strength, knowledge and, most importantly, love—love for my Self and all living life forms. I pledge from my heart to remain open to the flow of love from Spirit and focus this spiritual love in directions I may not have sent it in the past. I also promise to acknowledge the spiritual divinity that lies within each and every person I encounter on my journey.

I am so very grateful for all I have, all I will receive, and all I am able to give to others each day. I now read aloud the wishes for the coming year and those for this decade.

Read the birthday cylinder lists aloud.

If possible, at this time bury the lists in Mother Earth and say a private prayer. If not, place them on the altar so they will continually receive energy during the times you meditate and deliver your private prayer. Now complete the following exercise.

Journal Entries

I possess inner beauty because . . .

Truth can be found in . . .

Some of my wise qualities are . . .

Experience has taught me . . .

I know better than to ever again . . .

Life holds a new meaning because . . .

If I could have only one wish it would be . . .

What I now have to share that I didn't have five years ago is . . .

Ring the bell three times to conclude the ceremony.

This would be a good time to prepare some affirmation signs that you can place about your home in conspicuous areas. You started an energy flow with the ceremony, so allow it to carry on by creating a masterful treasure map that will bring your heart's desire into fruition. Details about treasure mapping can be found on page 16, if you need a refresher.

Many blessings await you!

Fifty

I feel that turning fifty is an event deserving reverence. It marks a new threshold of life for women—anything with "new" attached to it automatically signals to an empowered woman that something incredible is just around the corner that will lead her down a path designed to expose her to even grander adventures. This is unexplored territory; virgin, if you will. A woman of fifty symbolizes a person who has gone the distance, suffering bruises along the way for the wisdom she gained but ultimately standing with dignity. For all of these reasons and more, I have created a special ceremony in recognition of my sisters who are turning fifty and wish to share this ceremonial experience with other women. (If you happen to be a particularly shy lady, it is perfectly permissible to use the previous ceremony for turning forty instead of this one. I don't want to add any additional trauma to your life!) The tools you will need are as follows:

1. Your favorite incense for growth and creativity, like rose or lilac.
2. Select a pink candle for love of self and others; green for growth; blue for creativity and peace; white for purity; and three purple candles representing spirituality and wisdom.
3. Choose as many of the following stones as you own to wear and place on the altar: amethyst, aventurine, diamond, garnet, lapis, moonstone, opal, pearl, rock crystal, rose quartz, and turquoise.
4. A sacred object.
5. A small bell.
6. A dish of salt.
7. A bowl of water.
8. One white handkerchief or purple square of fabric, donated by a participant.
9. One green ribbon, contributed by a participant.
10. One small rock crystal, donated by a participant.
11. One white rose, brought by a participant.

12. Three coins (pennies are appropriate), donated by a participant.
13. A sacred article, such as a small cross, ankh, Star of David, or tiny Buddha statue, that is suited to your beliefs, also contributed by a participant.
14. A fireproof dish.
15. Birthday lists, tied with purple ribbons.

Begin with your normal morning routine and then build from there—be it gourmet coffee or orange juice while you enjoy the morning paper, make it a significant morning experience. Go the extra mile on this one. If you live in the city, order a sumptuous breakfast delivered to your door. Walk downtown to your favorite bagel shop to pick up a fresh blueberry delicacy. Perhaps your partner could be persuaded to prepare a queen's breakfast and serve it to you in bed. (Maybe they will crawl in with you!) Eat pancakes on the porch while you read the newspaper. Go to the beach with a breakfast picnic basket and watch the sun rise. Use your imagination!

At some point during the morning, compose two birthday wish lists. The first should be a listing of everything you wish to bring into reality within the coming year. The second list is for all those wonderful joys you wish to manifest in the next decade. Refer to page 15 under Affirmations if you need a refresher course on how to correctly phrase the desires. When the two lists are complete, roll them in a cylinder and tie each with a purple ribbon.

Cleanse your body with a bath oil, soap, or gel in the scent of rose. Play soft music while you bathe and be sure to burn three purple candles to set the mood. Wear something purple and loose-fitting.

Select three primary women who are special friends or relatives to assist in this ceremony; however, many more should be invited to attend and participate. All the women involved must bathe prior to the performance and wear either white or purple loose-fitting clothing. Everyone must be free from mind-altering influences.

The timing of the ceremony will probably depend upon when it is most convenient for everyone to assemble. If your birthday falls on a Wednesday, some of your friends may be working; therefore, an evening hour would be better suited. Should your birthday be on a Saturday when everyone is usually off from work, it would be best to schedule the ceremony during the morning hours. Morning is significant of birth, beginnings, and freshness.

Play soft music. Assemble all the tools on the altar before everyone arrives. As the women enter with their ceremonial gifts, have them place each one on the altar. When all the women have arrived, you and the three primary women should position yourselves so that you stand equally divided around the altar, forming the four anchors. The remaining women should stand in between so that you all form a circle that surrounds the altar. Decide among your three special friends who will be designated the first, second, and third primary woman.

Ring the bell three times to signal your ancestral guardians that the ceremony is about to begin.

The first primary woman lights the incense and then travels around the circle with it in hand, swirling the incense in a figure eight in front of each of the women assembled for the ceremony, beginning with the one being honored. Start at the head, then go to the center of the body and swirl down at the feet. Have each one turn around, repeating this cleansing action on the back of the body. The last person you cleanse should then cleanse you in the same manner. Return the incense to the altar. Assume your position within the circle.

One of the women gathered should light the pink candle, another the green candle, one the blue, and one the white. The three primary women are then to light one purple candle each. If there are not seven women present, have some light more than one candle, being sure to reserve the purple candles for the three primary women.

While soft music is playing, everyone should close their eyes, inhale deeply three times, and allow the music and atmosphere to still their minds and bodies. When it feels appropriate, the first primary woman should read the following passage:

> **Blessed Mother, it is with a joy-filled heart that I stand here for the purpose of honoring (name). She carries a wise heart within her bosom, full of compassion while heavy with experiences one**

would expect to have encountered by the age of fifty. Spirit has wisely blessed her with many joys and appropriate sadnesses so that she may experience balance and learn from the events of this Earth walk. May the angels now surround her like a golden ring of good fortune, shielding (name) from detours on this new journey. I pray for her vision to be as clear and bright as the new sun rising, and her days to be an ever-increasing abundance of blessed happenings. May (name)'s relationship with her ancestral females and spiritual guardians blossom more fully so that she may constantly feel their warm embrace as her new journey unfolds.

The second primary woman then reads the following:

Great Goddess, we ask that happy blessings be bestowed upon (name) as she enters this new decade of wisdom. Fill her wide pockets and outstretched hands with bountiful treasures sufficient for the queen she is. May her heart swell to capacity with the gentlest love for humankind, the animal kingdom, and our precious Mother Earth so that she may endow each with the unlimited generosity that Spirit has blessed upon her. Good Will and Mother Plenty shall walk beside (name) for all her days, guiding the distribution of the cornucopia with all who come upon her life path. Let her beautiful spirit be an example to others so that they too may know true happiness within the soul.

The third primary woman reads the following:

Ancestral women, bless your child with perfect health. Wrap her within your collective loving embrace so that she may always experience robust energy within her being. Bless (name) with a healthy heart, powerful mind, quicksilver wit, and a pure spirit,

so that she may go forth on this day and all others released from any hindering bonds that may inhibit her spiritual and personal development. Fill her physical body with the power of the agile panther, the stamina of the enduring camel, and the strength of a mother elephant's love. Allow this child of God to be ever empowered in body, mind, and spirit.

Read aloud your birthday list for the coming year. Touch the list to the flame of the green candle. Place the burning paper into the fireproof dish, saying aloud:

Beloved Mother, I give gracious thanks for the manifestation of my desires.

Have the woman who brought the rock crystal place it in the center of the cloth square, saying:

I bring this gift from the Goddess for the purpose of bestowing clear vision upon the physical eyes and spiritual mind.

The woman who donated the three coins should place them on the cloth, saying aloud:

These coins come from the gods, with the intention of attracting greater gifts of prosperity for sharing.

Read aloud the birthday list for the decade. Touch the list to the green candle flame, then place it in the fireproof dish to burn to ashes. Say aloud as it burns:

Thank you, blessed Goddess, for the manifestation of my wishes.

The woman who brought the sacred object should place it on the cloth at this time, saying:

May spirituality light your soul for all your days with peaceful understanding and awareness.

The second primary woman removes a petal from the white rose and places it in the bowl of water. This action should be repeated until there are seven petals floating on the water. Pass the bowl over the incense so the smoke will lift the vibration higher and then stand before the birthday girl. Bless her with the water by dipping two fingers into the bowl and then touching her third eye area (the forehead), saying aloud:

Blessed is this wise woman.

After the blessing, travel around the circle with the water bowl so that each of the women may bless themselves by placing two fingers into the water and touching their foreheads at the third eye area. An audible self-blessing may be spoken by each and is optional.

Return the bowl of water to the altar. Remove the remaining petals of the rose, placing each on the cloth, saying:

May the purity of love from the Goddess always and in all ways touch (name).

The third primary woman empties the dish of ashes from the birthday lists into the cloth, sprinkles all the articles contained within the cloth with a pinch of salt, and ties the four corners together with the green ribbon. Pass the bundle above the candles and through the smoke of the incense, saying:

**Highest is, highest does, wishes join together with spirits above.
Blessings mixed with desire, sail on smoke ignited by the power of fire.**

Give the blessing bundle to the birthday girl and return to your station within the circle.

The birthday girl, with the blessing bundle in hand and eyes closed, should now silently state your prayer of gratitude. When this has been completed, read aloud the following declaration:

> **Precious Mother, I am humbled by the spoken words in this ceremony. The sincerity of the prayers and declarations delivered by my sisters touches my heart at its deepest point. These women, dear Goddess, will be my sisters forever and always, for we are bound together with invisible ties that bond us spiritually. We share an enduring sister-love because we are eternally joined on this unique spiritual voyage. We are forever a part of the whole of this mystical entity that we form individually on this day. My heart overflows with gratitude for the blessings I have received from all of you.**
>
> **Within this circle of light and love, I am imbued with an all-empowering energy, created through the intensity of your emotions and good will. I feel this invincible power force emanating from within my being. I am in touch with my Creator, the power that manifested me, you, and all that is. As one leaf is a part of the whole oak tree, so am I a part of you, all that is, and thee. This energy force empowers my daily routine, creates my bountiful outcomes, and readies my future happenings. I stand tall in the knowledge that I create. I am a powerful woman. I am an invincible being. I am empowered.**
>
> **I am the daughter of (name), who is the daughter of (name), who is the daughter of (name). My ancestral mothers lovingly guide and fiercely protect my journey on this Earth plane. I give sincere thanks to those from the spirit side of life for their unending devotion, and am filled with heartfelt gratitude for all who extend their unconditional love as I travel my personal path. They are wise women. I am a wise woman. I am a wise woman. I am a wise woman.**

The woman who lit the pink candle should now extinguish it and say aloud:

Love encircles (name) forever and always.

The woman who lit the green candle should now extinguish it and say aloud:

Prosperity falls easily upon (name).

The woman who lit the blue candle should now extinguish it and say aloud:

(Name) is infused with creativity.

The woman who lit the white candle should now extinguish it and say aloud:

A pure heart and spirit belong to (name).

The first primary woman should extinguish one purple candle and say aloud:

Blessed is this woman.

The second primary woman should extinguish the next purple candle and say aloud:

Empowered is this woman.

The third primary woman should extinguish the final purple candle and say aloud:

Go forward this day a wise woman.

Ring the bell three times to conclude this ceremony.

The blessing bundle is a sacred article and should be cherished. Place it on your altar permanently.

Following the ceremony, you and all your spiritual sisters should to go out to celebrate in whatever manner is best suited to all of your tastes. Shopping! Lunch! The movies! All of the above! Have fun, be crazy, but most importantly, spend time together.

In the future, should a situation arise where you need to draw strength, inspiration, healing, or courage, my suggestion would be to hold the blessing bundle with both hands up to your heart chakra (that's the energy center located in the middle of your chest). Meditate on the blessing bundle, drawing its power into your chakra. Remind yourself repeatedly that Spirit is at work and a positive outcome will eventually manifest. Trust. Believe. Remain meditative for as long as it feels correct to do so. This should help to assist you in whatever circumstance that is troubling.

Go forth empowered!

When all the dust settles down, spend some time alone working with the following journal exercise.

Journal Entries

In the coming year I would like to improve my . . .

The ways I can be of better service to humankind are . . .

I have acquired the following talents to assist in this endeavor . . .

It is my heartfelt desire to . . .

I feel a stronger sense of empowerment because . . .

I am beautiful because . . .

What do wrinkles and gray hair signify to me?

Who has been most influential in my life?

How does this influence affect me now?

Now that I am fifty, I can give grateful thanks for . . .

Affirmations for Forty and Fifty

I possess the wisdom of the Goddess

I am filled with the love and understanding of Spirit

All my days are filled with love

I am Joy personified

Only goodness and happiness are attracted to me now

I am whole, healed, and happy

My heart's desire is attracted to me now

Goddess lights my path with a candle of love

Only goodness surrounds me now

The Heavenly Mother blesses all my circumstances

. . . Beyond

Each decade we reach brings a newness that is special to that time period. There is a shift in perspective, a newfound wisdom, and increasing personal confidence. We are wiser, stronger beings, seeing life through different eyes. The outer trappings and mundane issues of our day are viewed realistically. What is truly important to us is more clearly defined.

As with everything in life, nothing stays the same, although we may wish at times that it did. Many of us may think it would be great to be twenty-one forever. Well, on second thought, perhaps that's just a little too young. But maybe thirty-three—that's a great age to remain. Yes, but—what about forty-five? Many women are finding that forty-five is pretty cool nowadays. In our forties we have all that wisdom we have accumulated over the years and we are still physically agile. We're also young enough to have a big future in a new career. We can start all over now that the kids are in college or on their own. Yeah, forty-five is a pretty nice age. Of course, if we are sixty-five, fifty probably looks good. Hmm. You know, it is all a matter of perspective, isn't it? At sixteen, forty seems ancient. At seventy, twenty-one is a baby. Perhaps we should simply be happy to be where we are. We don't have any choice in the matter anyway . . . ladies, let us welcome each new decade with open arms!

As we age, I feel that it is crucial not to allow ourselves to adopt the attitude of considering ourselves to be old and therefore useless. What is old anyway? An antique mahogany table—which, as a society, we place great worth upon—would be considered old. Old can be a word associated with a village established in 1894. That would make that community historic. Old can be a philosophy that has continued to be valuable for a hundred years or more. Old can be grandma's soft cheek, the one the children love to nestle up close to. There are many wonderful aspects associated with things that are old chronologically, aspects that continue to provide knowledge, nurturing, happiness, and value. Once again, it is all in how we perceive it. Let's not devalue our worth, let us glorify it!

Let us glorify our age!

Why not enjoy all the mysteries that will unfold within the next decade? Why not anticipate with excitement what is yet to be? There is new beauty and grandeur within every experience we will encounter. Our beings will certainly gain greater magnificence upon entering the next decade. Let us embrace the coming years with appreciation, love, peace, and harmony within our souls. Let us thank God for this opportunity to dance to the melody of those who have traveled this road before us and continued to live a fruitful existence.

Just like a chocolate éclair, sometimes under all the crust we place protectively around us lies a delicate center. Edith, who was a neighbor of mine, could have fooled anyone—so confident, self-assured, and always knowing what to do in any situation. She had always been highly independent, supporting herself comfortably without assistance, never asking for another's advice. No one would have guessed that after she retired, Edith would cringe alone at home in silence. Flashbacks flooded her mind of when her mother had carelessly given Edith to neighbors and relatives to care for her needs. Weeks would pass by without her mother's presence. Alone and scared again, Edith was reliving those frightening childhood emotions.

Fortunately for Edith, she realized her behavior was destructive, so she sought advice. I gave her this ceremony to perform and a suggested reading list. Edith thought the ceremonial stuff was a little nuts at first, but she was willing to give it a try. She phoned me later to say that it had helped her to regain her focus and that she felt empowered once again. Her energy level had jumped skyward, and now she was looking to see what mischief she could get into! For years Edith had longed to be involved in the National Organization for Women. She realized that her dream could actually happen, now that she had the time available. Edith came to understand that she just needed to shift her energy in another direction, she still had volumes to share, and the best was yet to come.

The performance of this ceremony should be done at the beginning of each decade on the day of your birth when you have reached the age of sixty and beyond. If some quaky emotions arise halfway between decades, causing you to feel the need for a little reinforcement, then by all means celebrate your sixty-fifth or seventy-fifth birthday with this ceremony instead of the regular birthday ritual.

It is appropriate to spoil yourself on this day, as is the custom in all our birthday celebrations. To some, this may mean sleeping in a couple of hours longer or whipping up pancakes for breakfast. Maybe some sweet soul will serve you breakfast in bed. Indulge in a gourmet cup of coffee or your favorite tea. If juice is more appealing, drink that instead. While inhaling the aroma of the warm beverage or sipping juice, make a list of things you wish to accomplish in the coming year. Some may be whimsical, others practical, but especially list your heart's desire. Next, create a wish list for the decade. When writing your wishes, certain phrasing is more effective. If you need a refresher, please refer to page 15 under the heading Power Boosters, which addresses the most beneficial way to compose your wishes. When you have completed the lists, roll them into two cylinders and fasten them with a ribbon or hair tie. Set aside the lists to be used later during the ceremony.

Now take that scented, foaming bubble bath you have deserved for far too long—unless, of course, you don't have a tub. In that case, try a new shower gel in a delicious fragrance, purchased for this special occasion. While you luxuriate in your bath or shower, enjoy the peaceful sounds of soft music. If you are not going into work until much later, if at all (I would encourage the latter) or you are not employed, a glass of pink champagne might be in order, or a little champagne mixed with your orange juice. You may wish to experience all of this by candlelight. Do whatever pleases you—this is your day!

The bathing portion of your birthday recognition does not have to be followed by the ceremonial part. You may elect to separate these two segments by going shopping by yourself or with friends and enjoying a movie after the bath/shower experience, performing the ceremony when you return home. However, if you do follow your bathing with the ceremony, skip the champagne until dinner. The tools you will need to perform your birthday ceremony are:

1. An incense for love and healing, like rose.
2. Choose a pink candle for love; a green one for balance and healing; blue for inspiration; and three purple candles to reflect your spiritual nature.
3. Agate, amethyst, aventurine, bloodstone, citrine, diamond, emerald, garnet, jasper, lapis, malachite, moonstone, opal, pearl, peridot, rock crystal, rose quartz, and turquoise. Use all the stones or as many as you have in your possession. Wear them or place them on the altar.
4. A sacred object.
5. A dish of water.
6. A dish of salt.
7. A fireproof dish.

8. A small bell.
9. A journal and a pen.
10. Two birthday lists.

During the performance of this special ceremony it would be most beneficial to wear purple. If you do not have a garment in a natural fabric to wear in that color, white is acceptable.

Play soft music, light the candles and incense, and ring the small bell three times. Sit comfortably in front of the altar, either on the floor or in a chair.

Close your eyes and inhale deeply. Now visualize the smoke wafting up from the incense being drawn into your nostrils every time you inhale. See and feel the purifying smoke as it enters your body and begins to fill your head. Observe the smoke as it dances and floats around inside. With every breath, more purifying smoke is drawn into your being. Feel the clarifying energy as it gently descends into your neck and chest area, down into the arms and hands, into the torso and slides down the thighs, legs, and into the feet. See this beautiful healing energy as it twirls and dances around all your organs. Take your time. Now visualize this energy rising up from the floor, slowly and gently, encircling your body until you are completely encapsulated within the purifying smoke. Sit as long as you like within this healing energy while it works with your body. Relax. Enjoy. Take two deep breaths and read the following declaration:

> **Divine Mother, as I approach this new decade, I have no fear because I know within my heart that only the highest and best awaits me now. I trust in the realization that you have taken my hand and are guiding me through these coming years. Your presence has always been with me, as well as your love. I stand comfortably within the light that emanates from your spiritual being. I am forever shrouded within your heavenly reflection, protected, loved, and nurtured.**

Hold your birthday wish list for the year in your hand. Read the following prayer:

Dear Spirit, I ask most humbly that you bless these wishes of mine with white light energy, bringing them into manifestation now. I trust that my highest and best will be served as I read these wishes aloud. Amen. (Read the wishes aloud.)

Place the list next to the flame of the green candle to ignite it. Lay the burning paper in the fireproof dish. Say the following prayer:

Thank you, Goddess, for the manifestation of these wishes now. Amen.

Take the decade wish list into your hand and read the following prayer aloud:

Wise women in spirit, I respectfully ask that you direct my course through this next decade. Be my oarswomen as I sail into the coming years, steering me into only the safest of currents. Fill my sails with your holy breath so that I may succeed in all my endeavors. Be my anchor in times of turbulence, supporting me when I am unsure on my feet. And be my radiant suns, warming me with love always. I now read my wishes, hopes, and dreams for the coming decade. Amen. (Read the wishes aloud.)

Touch the decade wish list to the flame of one of the purple candles to ignite it. Place the burning paper into the dish with the other offering. Say the following prayer:

Thank you, Goddess, for the manifestation of these wishes now. Amen.

Read this prayer out loud:

> **Spiritual Mother, as the golden threads of my life continue to weave themselves into a tapestry of fulfillment, please allow me to be of sound mind, body, and spirit. Bless me with vibrant health that I may be agile, hearty, and filled with supreme energy. Grant me the clarity of mind so that I may function all of my days with the keen awareness of a child. Bestow upon me a bounty of inner wisdom and spiritual enlightenment so that I may know you more deeply. May I see through the clear eyes of those who have gone before me. May I hear with the divine hearing of those who are wiser. May I speak with the fluid tongue of those who are divine. May I continue to grow in the footsteps of the wise women.**
>
> **I open my Self now to receive all the glorious gifts that you have prepared for me. I give humble and grateful thanks for the harvest I am reaping. Spirit is good to me and has blessed me with a loving heart and joyful disposition. All my days shall be wondrous days filled with peace, health, love, and wisdom. I am so very fortunate to be me. Thank you, blessed Goddess, for making my dreams come true. Amen.**

Begin to extinguish all the candles. As you do so, after the flame has died on each, say:

> **Thank you, Goddess, for these manifestations now.**

Take the dish with the ashes of your wishes outside so you can bury the ashes, returning them to the Mother Earth to be nurtured. If this is not possible to do, allow them to float off into the wind to join with the universe to be blessed. Return to the altar and ring the bell three times to conclude the ceremony.

A journaling exercise has also been created for your further development. After you complete it, you may wish to create some affirmation signs. Give those beautiful hopes and wishes from your lists a boost of power by writing them on colorful paper. Place them about the house in areas where you will easily see them so you can continually jar your subconscious mind into manifesting your heart's desire!

Journal Entries

Of my accomplishments, I am most proud of . . .

I was able to accomplish this because I am . . .

One thing that has always gotten me through the rough spots is . . .

I know my future is bright because . . .

Each day is blessed because . . .

One of my most precious moments was . . .

The way I can continue to create precious moments is by . . .

Smile at the coming of the new decade!

Affirmations for Beyond

I am healthy, wealthy, and wise

I am filled with Divine Guidance

Goddess blesses my every endeavor

I am whole, healed, and happy

Love is the answer

Bountiful joys are mine now

I am grateful for all my experiences

Thank you, Goddess, I am growing

My arms lovingly embrace everyone

My wisdom is for sharing

Closure

Closing the Chapter

Opportunity crosses our paths everyday, sometimes clothed in unforeseen circumstances that eventually become bright, new potentials hiding within the loss of what we felt to be stable. This detour in our lives may be due to downsizing within the company we used to work for or the realization that a personal goal will never be brought to fruition. Whatever the case, at times like these, closure is considered by analysts to be beneficial for our well-being.

The ideal is to trust in the process by understanding that these situations manifest for our highest good. The universe, by springboarding us on to more magnificent adventures than we have encountered in the past, is

giving us an opportunity for expansion. Life is calling us forward. Our window of opportunity is shining brightly—just around the corner. But first we must put the old to rest. The following ceremony is designed for women who want to bring closure to a situation, condition, career—whatever the need. The entire ceremony should be read in advance of its performance.

Life is calling us forward

On the day you choose to perform this ceremony, please do so with a clear head and clean body, so do not contaminate your personal energy field with substances at this time. The cleansing of the body prior to the ceremony is a purification process. Along with creating a very relaxing atmosphere for yourself, you will also be washing away any barriers so that you will be a clear channel for spiritual energy. Use scented soap, gel, or bath oil to place you in a relaxed state of being through the power of aroma. Soft music playing is preferable while you bathe, and candlelight will add a mystical touch. Afterward, select a loose-fitting garment in a natural fabric in the color of white or blue to wear.

Assemble the following tools after you have read the entire ceremony:

1. Your incense of choice for good fortune, like cedar, lilac, or jasmine.
2. Use a green candle for prosperity; a yellow one to represent the intellect; and an orange candle for change. If you work in an artistic field, use a blue candle for creativity also.
3. Aventurine, emerald, snow quartz, and tourmaline. Use all the stones or as many as you have in your possession. Wear them or place them on the altar.
4. A tablet of paper and a pen.
5. A dish of water.
6. A dish of salt.
7. A fireproof bowl.
8. A small bell.
9. A journal.

Assemble your tools on the altar. Light all the candles and incense, play soft music, ring the bell three times to signal the beginning of the ceremony, and sit on the floor or in a comfortable chair in front of the altar. At this time, reflect on the circumstances that were within your control that brought you to this situation. Write your thoughts on the paper provided. Also make a list of lessons learned from this experience or what signs you ignored along the way that led to this conclusion. Take as long as you wish. When you are done, fold the paper(s) into quarters and place it on the altar for now.

Close your eyes and begin to center yourself by breathing deeply. Surround yourself with a beautiful ball of white light energy, above and below, to each side, in front and in back of yourself. Sit quietly, listening. Feel your energy expand. Realize you are within a protective cocoon of spiritual energy. You are Spirit's perfect child. Goddess loves you. The wonders that are manifesting for you are magnificent. No one can deny your highest and best good. It is your personal destiny to receive these divine gifts. Open yourself fully to receive what already is yours. Read the following prayer aloud:

> **Honorable Mother, I mistakenly thought I had lost what I perceived to be mine. I now realize that the gifts we hold are merely on loan to us for a period of time until their usefulness is spent. When circumstances arise to bring change, I now understand that it is time to move forward into a new adventure. Goddess has a higher plan for me. I know from my past experiences that when a door closes, another one is beginning to open. I may not see what is on the other side of that door just yet, but I do trust that beyond the sliver of light peeking around the door is a change for the better. I give grateful thanks for this experience and the lessons I have been shown.**
>
> **The time has come for personal growth. Spirit knows better than I when it is time to move ahead. My heart and mind are open to this new endeavor and I happily accept all the wondrous changes that are before me. I open wide my arms with**

expectation and embrace with complete trust the divine gifts I am receiving now. My cup of life is filled with heartfelt anticipation for my new adventure. I truly know I deserve the best that life can provide. As a child of God, I am well cared for. All my needs are divinely blessed into perfection. Only the highest and best is along my path this day and every day. My heart beats a joyful rhythm that corresponds to the music of my life. Amen.

Remove the folded paper from the altar. Touch it to the flame of the green candle, setting it afire, then place the burning paper in the dish, allowing it to burn down into ashes. Pick up the dish with the ashes and walk outside your dwelling. Allow the ashes to blow away. You are releasing the past, thus making room for goodness to enter in, creating a fresh start. If for some reason it is impossible to release the ashes this way, flush them down the commode. Go back inside and ring the small bell with a joy-filled heart to conclude the ritual.

Proceed ahead to the journal exercise.

Journal Entries

What did I learn from this situation?

What steps can I take to keep this from happening again?

Knowing what I know now, if this situation should happen again, what could I do to make it less painful?

The blessings I have received from this are . . .

I am grateful for . . .

I now will endeavor to . . .

My future is brighter because . . .

Anticipate the wonderful good fortune that is coming your way!

Affirmations for Closure

I see before me only bright, new beginnings

I am on the golden path to success now

Opportunity calls my name loudly

New fruitful journeys beckon to me now

My life is filled with love, success, and health

Spirit directs my highest and best good now

Goddess watches over me always and in all ways

I am eternally blessed by Spirit

Bestowed upon me now are the blessings of Spirit

I am happy, healthy, and whole

Releasing Relationships

The conclusion of a relationship, whether it is our choice or that of our partner, is an opportunity for personal growth. As in all cases of closure, this happens for our highest and best good. The objective is to continually focus ourselves on the positives associated with this event. We must trust that Spirit will unfold a deeper meaning for this experience and lead us through this portal into a new awareness of Self.

One important factor in bringing closure to a relationship is forgiveness. However difficult it may be to forgive transgressions against us, that is exactly what we must accomplish in our minds and eventually within our hearts. In the forgiveness of another, our soul—our spirit—is released from the bondage of contempt and set free to explore higher realities. It may also be necessary to forgive our own behavior. Carrying around a mound of guilt is not a healthy practice. Forgiveness benefits our spiritual and physical bodies and affects our mental outlook. It helps us push forward into our newness.

This ceremony is designed to benefit women who are in transition due to a breakup in an unmarried relationship. The next ceremony addresses divorce specifically.

Some years back, before I knew my present husband, I thought I had found the most perfect man. We shared an interest in the mysteries of the spiritual and psychic realms. I saw him becoming the next Edgar Cayce and me in the role of his faithful wife. When he ended our relationship, my whole life abruptly took a nasty turn. Not only was our relationship ending, I had to leave the house I loved and find an apartment to live in that I could afford. I was devastated. I went about my days of packing, tearfully trying to understand what had happened.

During the sad times I spent alone in my new apartment initially, I journaled. I wrote long, emotional entries, spilling my little heart onto the pages of my journal while my tears splashed onto the paper. I remember writing over and over six words: *Thank you, God, I am learning.*

The ending of this particular relationship taught me many lessons that I have valued greatly through the years. By using the journaling process, I was able to see why our relationship had failed. I had been so blinded by my neediness, his manipulations, and what I chose to call love that I was incapable of seeing reality. Placing pen to paper helped me immensely to get my head back on straight. I was blessed to have had the wisdom to change my negative perspective to one that was positive. And as time went by, I became much stronger under my own power.

As I often say, once we are to a point in time where we can reflect back, we will easily see why things did not work out and be very grateful that they didn't. I can honestly say that I would not be the woman I am today if I had married that man. I am very thankful he ended that unhealthy relationship, for whatever reason. Was his behavior forgivable? Certainly. I lost nothing and gained many blessings from the experience.

Read the entire ceremony first so you will be acquainted with the process. Once you have read the ceremony, you will see that it is necessary to allot ample time for completion and be in the right frame of mind to achieve the intended results.

Prepare yourself by cleansing your body prior to the ceremony. In this manner you will wash away any barriers that may hinder you from being a clear channel for spiritual energy. Use scented soap, gel, or bath oil to place you in a relaxed state of being through the power of aroma. Soft music playing is preferable while you bathe, and candlelight will add a mystical touch. Sobriety is also important so as not to contaminate your personal energy field with substances at this time. After you have bathed, select a loose-fitting garment in a natural fabric in the color of white or pink to wear.

The following tools are necessary:

1. Choose an incense that reflects peace, love, harmony, and healing, like lavender or rose.
2. The candles should represent peace, love, and healing. I would suggest blue, pink, and green.
3. Aventurine, citrine, garnet, malachite, moonstone, and rose quartz. Use all the stones or as many as you have in your possession. Wear them or place them on the altar.
4. A sacred symbol, if desired.
5. A dish of water.
6. A dish of salt.
7. A tablet and a pen.
8. A large fireproof ceramic or glass dish.
9. A gentle bell.
10. A box of tissues.
11. A journal.

Light the candles and incense, play soft music, and ring the bell to begin the ceremony. Sit in front of the altar either on the floor or in a chair. Quiet yourself. Close your eyes and breathe deeply, in and out, in and out. Visualize a brilliant pink light in the center of your chest. Feel God's healing love warming you. See your love light shine brilliantly and watch as the pink light emanates from within, shooting rosy rays of light energy outward. As God's child, you are filled with love. Love is your natural companion. Take a deep breath and open your eyes. Read the following declaration:

> **Infinite Spirit, my true nature is to feel love and happiness. When I am in touch with my heart center, I feel love, I am whole, and I am open to truth. I hear clearly the messages from my Self. God's love is present everywhere I look—in all people, situations, and possibilities. When I ignore my heart center, I blind myself to truth. I cannot see the goodness that lies in all people and events, or recognize opportunities. My emotions cloud the vision of reality.**
>
> **I know I must remove any obstacles that block my spiritual path. The time has come to release from my spirit any feelings that would impede my journey. I am a forgiving person. I know in my heart this is the correct action for me in this situation.**

Having concluded the reading of the declaration, write in the tablet the emotions you still hold about this person that are not for your highest and best good. Express any feelings of betrayal, hurt, abandonment, or guilt, whatever is appropriate in your particular situation. The purpose here is to release any ill will or guilt you may feel in your heart, using the vehicle of the written word so that you may step forward as a renewed, enlightened woman. Take as long as is necessary to accomplish this release process, using all the sheets of paper and tissues you require.

Tear out the sheets of paper from the tablet, fold everything into quarters, touch the paper to the green candle flame to ignite, then place it in the ceramic or glass dish. As the paper burns to ashes, say this prayer aloud:

Heavenly Mother, I cleanse and purify these emotions with fire, thus releasing my attachment to them. As these sentiments float upward to the ethers, I ask that they be transformed into feelings of forgiveness. Please open my heart to a new understanding of this situation and bring me compassion and love. Amen.

Compose a letter of forgiveness on another sheet of paper. Some women may find it difficult to genuinely express forgiveness at this moment, while others will not. With continuing effort, everyone should eventually achieve an understanding of forgiveness. Even if the words are not sincerely felt at this time, write them down. This is the beginning of the healing process for you. Remember, we must take baby steps before we can run. You will feel true forgiveness in your heart soon. When this happens, a healing will have taken place in your soul and an upliftment will be experienced in your spirit. Again, take as long as you need to complete your letter.

When the forgiveness letter is finished, fold it into quarters. Wave the folded letter over the incense so the smoke can purify it and raise the energy. Hold the letter between your palms to bless it. Say a private prayer for the person you have forgiven, even if it is yourself, asking for the highest and best good. Touch the letter to the pink candle flame to ignite it. Place the burning letter in the dish along with the other paper that has turned to ashes. Make this declaration aloud:

May these words float gently upon the smoke and evoke fond blessings in my heart, soul, and spirit.

Take several deep breaths. Read aloud the following prayer:

My heart is open to understanding events in my life that contribute to my personal spiritual growth. I am capable of seeing the wisdom in all my experiences. I stand ready to receive this enlightenment now. I trust in the Goddess to be my steadfast companion, my everlasting support, in all matters. In silence I

> **speak my heart and listen for the gentle response I know will follow. I rest easy in the knowledge that Spirit loves me. Only goodness can come to me now. I am grateful for this opportunity for spiritual expansion. Thank you, Spirit, I am growing! Amen.**

Take the dish of ashes and either sprinkle them outside on the ground or allow them to float in the air. If this is impossible for some reason to complete, flush the ashes down the commode. Say a private prayer of thanksgiving for this experience in life. Return to the altar and ring the gentle bell three times to conclude the ceremony.

At this time you will find it comforting and enlightening to continue on to the journaling segment.

Journal Entries

I can forgive because I am . . .

The obvious reason(s) our relationship did not work out is . . .

I am grateful to Spirit for this opportunity to grow because . . .

The strengths I have gained that I will now bring into the next relationship are . . .

Three blessings that I would wish upon this person are . . .

For the next week, continue to journal your thoughts and emotions. What comes from these writings may be very beneficial and revealing.

A client of mine found that she was able to genuinely forgive her boyfriend during the ceremony; however, the pain of his rejection remained. Through the continuing journaling process in the week that followed, she was able to heal her heart. My client discovered a pattern in all her relationships that caused the eventual breakups. She came to realize that she was the creator of the problem and, therefore, was the only one who could correct it. This recognition showed her that she was in control of her destiny and gave her empowerment.

Sing with gratitude!

Affirmations for Forgiveness

Thank you, Spirit, for this opportunity to grow

I am blessed with the wisdom of the wise women

Goddess blesses every step I now take

Only happiness stands before me now

My soul is filled with Goddess light

Spirit guides all my new relationships

The eternal mother loves me in all ways and always

I trust in the Goddess to heal my heart and
create a new understanding now

Love is the answer

I forgive myself

The Divorce

It should come as no surprise to anyone reading this book that in our modern society divorce happens to fifty percent of married couples. Therefore, it is appropriate to include a ceremony for women who are in the process of divorce. Having personally experienced the emotional pain that a failed marriage can bring, I know the vulnerability women feel and the frequently accompanying fear of the future. And, of course, if children are involved, the problems are magnified.

Women may feel that their socially acceptable role has been exchanged for a lesser status, that of an unmarried "failure," which may create self-esteem problems. Many are thrown into a panic because they feel they "need"

a man emotionally and are convinced they cannot survive alone. Then there are women who swear they will never marry again, all men are scum. It is also not uncommon for women who are devastated by the departure of their spouses and filled with jealous anger to entertain thoughts of revenge.

A female acquaintance of mine some years ago used her son unmercifully to aggravate her ex-husband. Every time John came to her house to pick up Danny for a weekend visit, Sherry would always have some final preparation work to do, such as bathing the child, dressing him, or packing his overnight bag. Sometimes these delays would last an hour. Once John began dating another woman regularly, the problem escalated. Whenever Sherry was scheduled to deliver the child to John's house, she was always late, frequently ruining his plans. After John remarried, she became even more difficult to deal with, constantly complaining on the phone about one problem or another she was having with their son, who, in my estimation, was a well-behaved child. Sherry would also call often to ask for his advice on matters relating to the house she had received in the divorce settlement or what kind of a new car she should buy. Naturally, these frequent phone calls caused great annoyance for the new wife.

We all know someone like Sherry. However, if her behavior is similar to yours, then this chapter will set you free from the bondage of revenge.

Everyone reacts individually to divorce, and we are certainly entitled to have our share of evil thoughts, mean-spirited words, less-than-attractive tantrums, and major crying jags. But, in the long run, no matter who is at fault, no useful purpose can be served by creating havoc in the other's life. If revenge is on our minds, we must realize this is an anger-based emotional response that is not worthy of the spiritually empowered woman. Only harmful outcomes can manifest from anger. We do not want to go there.

If there are children involved in the divorce, the appropriate action is to consider their welfare first instead of how hurt you are. After all, they are not divorcing their father, you are. He will remain their dad forever, as it should be. It will be necessary to rise above this circumstance because you are setting an example for your children to follow, that of how people treat each other under the worst of circumstances. Your husband may be acting like a jerk, or has in the past, but that doesn't give you license to behave that way toward him. Rise above, don't lower yourself, and your children will respect you. It's also helpful to remember the uncanny ability children have for seeing through people. If your husband has behaved badly, they know it. Don't follow his example.

Even when it is not readily apparent to us, it is important to remember that everyone, *everyone*, has a beautiful soul. The outer person may have offended us, but the inner being is still a perfect spirit. During the divorce process and after, when your ex comes to the door for his visitation with the children, it may be difficult to see him. Every time you encounter your former mate, it is best to focus on that perfect inner soul so you will manifest a speedy healing. I would suggest thinking repeatedly while in his presence, "I honor your beautiful soul." The difference will be immediately felt inside your spirit and perhaps his spirit as well.

Thank you, God, I am learning

I believe it is possible to have a "positive divorce" if the art of forgiveness is practiced. I realize that certain behaviors are unconscionable and do not hold any redeeming value; nevertheless, we must focus on the positive lesson presented to us rather than the horrible demonstration we were shown. Over time, good is born from bad. As difficult as it may be, eventually you must reach a level of forgiveness. If that sounds like an impossibility, try seeking a new understanding. You can consciously choose to view any situation in your life through different eyes. That doesn't mean you are required to agree with the former behavior, it simply means you can see it differently, through understanding. And with enough passage of time, eventually true forgiveness is possible to accomplish.

The whole point here is to create a healthier, happier attitude about the divorce, and through the performance of ceremony you will manifest that perception into reality. Even if you are just going through the motions at this time, you will feel lighter and relieved of a portion of the burden you are carrying.

I would recommend performing this ceremony on the actual day the divorce is final, or at least within the next day or two. The final divorce decree signals an ending but, as with other situations in life, endings are also new beginnings. The desirable action is to welcome the new into your life as soon as possible. Therefore, the sooner you perform the ceremony, the better for your well-being.

If you happen upon this book shortly after your divorce, or are still harboring major feelings of animosity years later, it would benefit you immensely to perform this ceremony. Those emotions need to be healed, so cleanse the grief away, even if it is years later.

Throughout the process of reaching a settlement on custody, support, and visitation rights, I would strongly suggest the benefits of journaling. This is the perfect vehicle in which to release the pent-up anger and hostile emotions that are fermenting within. Write letters in your journal to your spouse filled with all the unwanted emotions you are living with. Just don't tear out the pages and mail them! Safely pour into your journal all the ugliness and nasty feelings dwelling inside. By the time the divorce decree is signed, you could be rid of most of that negativity. This procedure will also help you to maintain a calmer demeanor when you are in the presence of your spouse. Remember, this is to benefit your children. If you don't have children, it will benefit your soul.

When you perform this ceremony, afterwards plan to treat yourself, at the very least, to dinner out. Why not go to that restaurant you and all of your girlfriends have been dying to try? Have a glass of champagne to toast your newfound freedom and upcoming adventures. If it is possible to squeeze in some pamper time, do that too. Ask a friend to take the kids for the day so you can play—she'll understand. Have your nails done, schedule a massage, or call your beautician to create a new hairstyle. Spoil yourself; you deserve it! Remember to read the entire ceremony in advance of its performance.

The tools needed for the divorce ceremony are as follows:

1. Jasmine incense for balance, peace, and love.
2. Choose an orange candle for change; green for renewal, healing, and balance; pink for self-love; white for purity; and purple for spiritual wisdom.
3. Agate, amethyst, aventurine, citrine, fluorite, jet, malachite, moonstone, rock crystal, rose quartz, and tourmaline. Use all the stones or as many as you have in your possession. Wear them or place them on the altar.

4. A gentle bell.
5. A dish of water.
6. A dish of salt.
7. A sacred object, if desired.
8. A journal and a pen.

Preparation for this ceremony is important. You will want to literally and figuratively cleanse your body of the negatives of the day or years of leftover emotions. This purifying process is necessary in order to wash away any barriers so that you will be a clear channel for spiritual energy. A bubble bath with a deliciously scented rose bath oil is the optimum. Two tablespoons of sea salt added to the bath water will contribute greater cleansing benefits. If you do not have a tub, use a rose-scented bath soap or gel. You could mix small amounts of sea salt with the lather for additional cleansing. Play soft music and have pink candles burning. When you have completed your relaxing cleanse, wear a loose-fitting garment in a natural fabric that is in the color of white or pink.

Light all the candles and incense, play soft music, and sit in your chair or on the floor facing the altar. Ring the bell three times to signal the beginning of the ritual. Take a series of deep breaths, slowly in and steadily back out, everything in equal measure. Observe the pink candle. Watch the flame dance and flicker as you continue with a steady, easy breath. Memorize the image, then close your eyes. Visualize the candle and radiant flame dancing behind your closed eyes. Feel as if you are a part of the fire—the flame and you are one. Feel the warmth it generates permeate your body. Be conscious of this warming energy at the top of your head, slowly folding over your face, neck, back, and chest, and flowing down into your hips and buttocks. Let the fire energy continue to enter your thighs, legs, ankles, and feet. The flame is cleansing all impure energy, negative emotions, and distraught feelings that are carried within your being. Now take a few deep breaths, open your eyes, and read this declaration:

Precious Spirit, I sit before you ready to embark on a new journey. The old one has come to an end, which may not have been

my original plan, but is still the reality of my life. I know that when situations present themselves, it is not by accident or coincidence. It is by divine design that I have been blessed with this new challenge in my life. I have learned uncountable lessons on my previous journey, and for that I am truly grateful. I am stronger, wiser, more mature, and better for this experience. But it is time to move on with my development, to reach further inside, to extend my Self outward. Life is about growth, and there is nothing more here to learn. I raise my hands in honor of this choice and recognize the wisdom held within this circumstance.

Dear Spirit, I ask that you remove from my heart any animosity that I carry for my spouse that may still remain within. Please render me incapable of any pettiness, hatred, or vengeance. I am a child of God; therefore, I am filled with forgiveness. My heart cannot entertain malice, only love. I honor the spirit of my husband, for it is pure spiritual energy, perfect, as is the Spirit of God. I feel only compassion within my bosom for this man. I know that he did the best he could with the understanding he possessed at this time in his life. I recognize that my spouse is on his own personal path and has his own unique challenges to overcome. He will make mistakes and grow from them, as I do from my own. He is no better than me, he is no less. He is simply different. It is not correct spiritually to pass judgment on him. The choices he made were not mine to make, so I must honor his perfect right to choose his destiny. I cannot and would not dictate how another should conduct their life, for that is a decision only they can make. His path is not the same as mine, but I am grateful that our paths crossed during our individual walks of life and am evermore thankful to have shared this experience with him. As we part, I bid him future

happiness, unlimited blessings of growth and understanding, and the wisdom to redirect his energy in a positive manner into his new realm of existence.

At this time, write a letter of forgiveness in your journal to your former spouse. Even if the words are not truly felt presently, create the letter anyway. Focus the letter only on his positive attributes, perhaps directing it in a flattering manner, such as, "I always found your patience admirable." Then write the words of forgiveness for whatever transgressions you feel he inflicted on you. *I forgive you for not listening to me. I know you did not realize how important it was for me to be heard by you. I forgive you for being insensitive to my needs. Given your childhood, you probably reacted as you were programmed to.* Finally, send him off with the hope he will eventually understand himself more clearly and grow from his participation in the marriage. *It is my truest desire that you will come to realize how to be a man who is sensitive to the needs of others.* Sign and date the letter and do not mail it. On occasion, you may feel supported by reading this letter if you start to resent your new situation or are frustrated by your previous spouse's continued loutish behavior.

Now, recite this prayer aloud:

Infinite Spirit, enfold me within your loving embrace so I may be sheltered by divine energy as I place my feet on this new path. I am a child of God. I am a beautiful soul. I possess great strength and wisdom, true compassion and understanding, and boundless love for all. Realizing that the Goddess is my guide, I know I am embarking on what can only be a magnificent journey. My future falls gently before me, laden with more opportunities than I can imagine at this time. I have a new destiny calling to me now. Fortune is singing merry tunes in my ear and promising wondrous adventures, unlike any I have previously experienced. My cup is overflowing with the gifts of hope, happiness, health, and harmony. I know not what glorious adven-

tures await me, but I place my trust in the process because I know everything is in divine order. Amen.

Extinguish the orange candle and say:

My heart is open to receive all the goodness that awaits me.

Put out the green candle and say:

I am physically renewed, emotionally healed, and my life is now in balance.

Extinguish the pink candle, saying:

I am a special, unique woman and no one like me has ever lived before, nor will again.

Put out the purple candle and say:

Thank you, Goddess, for this experience and the wisdom I am gaining.

Extinguish the white candle, saying:

My thoughts are filled with understanding.

Ring the bell three times to conclude the ceremony.

Journal Entries

I am proud of handling myself with dignity when . . .

The most important lesson I have learned through this divorce process is . . .

I know this is for my highest and best good because . . .

Now, if I should notice negative thoughts creeping into my consciousness, I will . . .

Three positive things my former husband taught me are . . .

I know the Goddess is leading the way on this new journey because . . .

One benefit I have received by practicing forgiveness is . . .

I am going to spoil myself with something nice:

I would strongly suggest daily journaling as a tool to strengthen forgiveness, especially if you had difficulty in expressing genuine forgiveness during the ceremony. Remember, the objective ultimately is complete forgiveness. You must forgive in order to heal your soul and uplift your spirit. Until you reach the point where you no longer feel animosity, revenge, or emotional pain, continue journaling. If you have to journal in the morning and the evening, do it. All those angry words, broken emotions, and vengeful acts must be replaced with true forgiveness, no matter how awful you think your former spouse is. This period of time after the performance of the ceremony is critical—it is when you will ripen. Those words written in the journal, when reread, will reveal many secrets. Lessons learned from journaling will assist in your spiritual and personal development. Those lessons will help you to gain empowerment.

Open your arms to happily embrace your new life!

Embrace your new life!

Affirmations for Divorce

I am blessed with a forgiving heart

The Goddess brings to me only happiness

Thank you, God, I am learning

My cup is overflowing with the gifts of hope, happiness, health, and harmony

I am Forgiveness personified

I see the spark of God within everyone

I give gracious thanks for this opportunity to grow

New opportunities shine like the sun for me now

God's white light shines all around me

I am a beautiful soul

Beginnings

The Wedding

As little girls we all probably had fairy tales read to us. Those charming stories unfortunately implanted into some of our psyches the illusion that when we grew up, Prince Charming would enter our lives, whisk us off our feet, and carry us away to live happily ever after. Somewhere along the way to ever after we were told that it was desirable to have two children, preferably a boy first and then a girl.

Although the husbands of my friends are quite nice, I would not classify any of them as Prince Charming (that would be an impossible ideal). Some of the women I associate with are not married, nor do they have children. In our current society the reality is that many women

do not expect a man to rescue them. Women make conscious choices to marry, or not, and to have children, or not. And sometimes they choose to have children without benefit of marriage. Others may be hesitant to marry again because of a disastrous marriage (or two) in the past, which can certainly make one a wee bit cautious to leap into the promise of marital bliss. We may also find ourselves defying convention by marrying late in life for the first time or the third. The beauty here is that we have freedom of choice without stigmas. This is our reality, not a fairy tale.

Wherever you are on your path, if you feel that the right partner has finally entered your life, and you both agree that wedding bells are on the horizon, then marriage is your status of choice. Weddings are one event I love to attend and truly enjoy officiating. The emotions and excitement that a couple feels at this time is unlike any other experience. The anticipation of all the new and beautiful opportunities that these two individual people will face together is overwhelming—in a nice way. Everyone can feel the energy that surrounds the happy couple long before the special day arrives. It is a time pregnant with the promise of hopes and dreams being fulfilled at long last. Yes, weddings are a joy.

The white light of God surrounds us

I feel it is important for a woman to prepare herself for her marriage through the act of ceremony. Marriage is an important event on anyone's path. We want to step out with the right foot, filled with positive thoughts but also carrying a realistic view. This ritual is intended to be a time for reflection, meditation, and the projection of your desires.

It is appropriate to schedule the performance during the week of and prior to the wedding. If you have planned a spectacular wedding, this may sound like one more thing to do amid the chaotic atmosphere of finalizing all the preparations for the big day. If that is your situation, I would suggest the week before. The hour you choose is not important; however, schedule the event when you have a sober head and sufficient time to bathe leisurely before the ceremony.

The items you will need to perform this ceremony are:

1. Rose or gardenia incense for love.
2. A pink candle for love; red for endurance; green for prosperity in all areas; and gold or yellow for change.
3. Amethyst, aventurine, emerald, jasper, jet, malachite, moonstone, pearl, rock crystal, rose quartz, snow quartz, sapphire, and tourmaline. Use all the stones or as many as you have in your possession. Wear them or place them on the altar.
4. A dish of water.
5. A dish of salt.
6. A sacred object, if desired.
7. One red rose.
8. A special handkerchief or a crystal bag, normally used for carrying stones.
9. A journal and a pen.
10. A small bell.

On this special ceremonial day, prepare yourself with great attention to detail. Have two pink candles to light the bathing area, burn rose or gardenia incense, and use rose bath oil or a gel if you have a shower. Play very romantic music, whatever sets your heartstrings to vibrating. Take as long as you desire—relaxing, languishing in the bubbles, or enjoying the water running over your body. After you have toweled off, wear a loose-fitting garment made from a natural fabric in the shade of pink.

At the altar, light all the candles and incense, play soft music, and ring the bell three times to begin the ceremony. Sit in a chair or on the floor facing the altar. Close your eyes. Inhale deeply through your nostrils and exhale through slightly parted lips. Repeat this action two more times. Now visualize a radiant, pink ball of light at the center of your chest. See it the size of a silver dollar. Feel the warmth emanating from the glow of the pink light. Slowly, allow the radiant light to expand, continually feeling its warmth on your body as it increases in size. See and feel the pink light grow larger and larger, in small increments, until it totally surrounds your body. Sit for a moment within the radiant light of love. Drink in its properties. Now read aloud the following declaration:

> **Infinite Spirit, I sit before you with a joy-filled heart. My wedding day approaches soon, and following it will come many grand adventures to be shared with my new husband. I stand eager to begin this journey, knowing that you will guide our path through me. I place my trust in your wisdom, conscious that it has never failed me. My senses are strong, perhaps even stronger for this union coming, and I will feel your continuing love and direction as my husband and I enter into matrimony. I know you will stand behind me as I speak my vows, blessing our union on that day and all days thereafter. It is with such unspeakable emotion that I give grateful praise and gratitude for this wondrous experience. Glorious is my wedding day! Beautiful is my marriage! Holy is our union!**

At this time, complete the following exercise.

Journal Entries

On my wedding day, I wish . . .

It is my desire that our marriage will bring . . .

I want us to share . . .

It is my wish that we create together . . .

My hope is for us to achieve together . . .

I bring to this marriage . . .

Love is a power, and I will use this force to bring . . .

What will hold our marriage together is . . .

Even though I know that I am perfect in spirit, I could endeavor to correct . . .

In ten years I can see us . . .

Once you have completed the journal entry, read aloud the following prayer:

Heavenly Mother, I ask for blessings of peace within our home, prosperity to weight our pockets, happiness to increase daily, and love to fill our hearts unceasingly. I ask for the wisdom to admit when I am wrong, the honesty to always tell the truth, the willingness to compromise, the ability to laugh at myself, and the talent of truly listening to what my partner says. I ask for an understanding and loving heart. Let me not be hasty to judge, but rather feel with wisdom. Allow my spirit to see beyond the obvious so that I may know true compassion. Let the bells ring within my heart the merry melody of faith in my spouse. Never let me doubt, always help me to know. Amen.

Take the red rose in your hand. Smell its lovely aroma and feel the softness of the petals with your fingertips. Study the red rose. This precious flower is symbolic of everlasting love. Place the handkerchief or crystal bag in your lap. Gently remove one red petal and place it in the center of the handkerchief or bag. As you place the petal in the container, do so in a contemplative manner. Think about what marriage really means, not just the glitz of your dress and all the fancy trappings that will accompany the service. Think about what you want to personally bring into this union that will benefit the relationship and your spouse, how you intend to make both of your lives better. Continue this contemplation as you pluck the petals from the rose, depositing them into the hanky or bag. Symbolically you are projecting positive energy and good will into the relationship. When you have removed all the petals from the rose, either fold the hanky or close the bag to contain the symbology of the petals. Wave the hanky/bag over the incense and candles so the smoke will bless the contents. Say aloud the following request:

Angelic beings, bless our love and marriage. Place it within a protective bubble of holy energy, eternally nourished by the Godforce.

Place the hanky or bag on the altar. Make the following declaration aloud:

> **Great Goddess, I give grateful thanks for my spouse-to-be. I recognize that I am fortunate to have found a wonderful soul to share my life. I dedicate myself now to being all that I can be in this marriage. The wedding vows are a sacred commitment, and I will state them with heartfelt sincerity. Everything happens for a reason and I trust in the guidance that has led me onto this path. Only good will manifest from this union. Together we will grow spiritually and experientially as we journey down life's pathway. Wisdom will be our friend and constant companion. Blessings will fill our lives and enrich others as we share our prosperity. Understanding and patience will create a bond that will strengthen us as a couple and individually. Communication will be easy and frequent, because I realize this is the life-blood of any relationship. Many will be our years together as we travel hand in hand through all obstacles on our joined pathway; may they be few. Thank you, Goddess, for this wondrous blessing of shared love.**

Snuff out the flame of the pink candle, saying:

> **Thank you, Heavenly Mother, for our love.**

Extinguish the flame of the red candle, saying:

> **I am grateful to the Goddess for this everlasting love.**

Snuff out the flame of the green candle, saying:

> **I thank you, Spirit, for our bounty.**

Extinguish the flame of the yellow or gold candle, saying:

Gracious Mother, I give humble thanks for our new joined pathway.

Ring the bell three times to conclude the ceremony. Find a place to reverently store the rose petals. This could be inside a book of scriptures, such as the Bible, or a special book of love poems. If the petals are enclosed within a bag, they could sit beside a special picture of the two of you, and later be placed beside a wedding picture. Whatever feels correct to you is the best plan.

Open your arms to true love!

Affirmations for Marriage

God watches over our union

I easily speak my feelings

Goddess blesses our union each day

Love flows easily from me to thee

It never hurts to laugh

Prosperity is attracted to our home

Opportunity knocks frequently in our lives

Love is the glue that bonds us together

I am Understanding personified

The white light of God surrounds us

A Baby Arrives

Becoming a mother is one of God's true blessings in life. For those maternally inclined, this is the ultimate experience, a dream come true. This is not to say that all woman should have children or to insinuate that there is something lacking within one who does not have the desire to produce offspring. It should be understood that becoming a mother is a personal decision. When contemplating such a momentous, life-changing event, we need to arrive at the conclusion independently of relatives' and friends' promptings and viewpoints.

If it is your desire to bear or adopt a child, I would encourage you to do so when the conditions are most favorable for the baby's benefit. Under normal circumstances, that would mean when you can afford the expense of another mouth to feed and have emotional and financial support from the father. If you are a financially secure professional woman who has a desire to give birth or adopt a child, but find no need for a father, emotionally or financially, then your considerations are different. The important issue here is that the decision to bring a precious life into your world is done with total regard for the ultimate benefit of the child. If everything is in alignment, and Spirit prompts you to create or adopt, then let nature take its course.

Children require great patience and limitless love. If you focus primarily on all the positive attributes associated with motherhood, such as the laughter, playfulness, complete trust, and love, rather than the more stressful conditions that will accompany your bundle of joy, you will be able to rise above any challenges and be a great mother. This is not to say one should enter into motherhood wearing rose-colored glasses—quite the opposite! I am merely trying to convey, as I have throughout this book, the message to look for the positive when times are rough. As you apply medicine to the affected area of diaper rash amid the child's voluminous cries, remember the peals of laughter that also emanate from your little angel.

The timing of the ceremony to recognize the impending birth of your baby or the adoption of a child is up to you to decide. Some women are so excited by the news of the birth after a confirming test or adoption process that they elect to perform the ritual shortly after, while others prefer to wait until they are in the second trimester or nearer to the actual adoption. Close to the time of delivery is another option, and a popular one, but if there is a possibility of entering into labor early, you could miss the opportunity entirely. If you are adopting a baby, I would suggest timing the ceremony near the anticipated birth, if you know it, or just prior to receiving the baby. In the case of adopting an older child, schedule the ceremony just prior to the child entering into your life.

Two sisters I know were pregnant with due dates that were within days of each other. Since they felt a special bond because of the similar timing of their pregnancies, they decided to perform the ceremony together. Ellie and Evelyn prepared two altars side by side in Ellie's home early in the morning after their husbands had gone to work. They synchronized their motions as best they could and spoke as one when delivering the declarations and prayers out loud. Ellie and Evelyn couldn't resist chuckling when they exposed their tummies during the belly blessing segment. Afterward, both reported that they felt an intensified psychic connection with their babies after the performance of the ritual.

Goddess blesses me and my baby

When you have selected the time you feel comfortable with, arrange to perform the ceremony as early as possible in the morning. Sunrise is preferable because it is the birth of a new day. I have created two ceremonies, one for the pregnant mother and one for the adopting mother. Read the entire ceremony that is appropriate for your situation first and collect the necessary tools. The preparation and tools are the same for both ceremonies. Where it changes is when you begin the performance. The items you will need for both rituals are as follows:

1. An incense for love such as jasmine, rose, patchouli, musk, gardenia, or vanilla.
2. Use a pink candle for love; white for purity; green for prosperity; and blue for creation.
3. Amethyst, aventurine, bloodstone, emerald, jasper, malachite, pearl, rock crystal, rose quartz, sapphire, and turquoise. Use all the stones or as many as you have in your possession. Wear them or place them on the altar.
4. A dish of salt.
5. A dish of water.
6. A sacred object, if desired.
7. A small bell.
8. A journal and a pen.
9. One pink rose and some baby's breath.
10. Small white cloth or a handkerchief spread open on the altar.
11. One pink ribbon and one blue ribbon.

Pregnant Mother

Rise early on the morning of the ceremony. Be sure to allot enough time to bathe prior to the ceremony, even if it is still dark outside. Soft music, a pink candle and a white candle, and rose-scented incense should accompany the bath. Use rose bath oil or gel, depending on whether you have a tub or shower, to bathe with. When you have finished bathing, wear a loose-fitting garment in the color of pink or white that is a natural fabric.

Light all the candles and incense on the altar and play music that is a little livelier than you would normally use, something with a distinctive rhythm—Celtic or Native American music would do nicely. Ring the bell three times to begin the ceremony.

While standing in front of the altar, focus your eyes on the flame of the green candle. Watch it dance and sway about. Become one with the candle, allowing it to draw you in. Feel your body as it sways to the rhythm of the music. Allow yourself to be free and loose, swaying with the melody, to and fro, gently. Let your arms come out to your sides and rise above your head, delicately waving your hands about in the air. Do whatever the music wills with your body. Continue to move with the music for as long as you wish. When you tire, sit on the floor or on a chair in front of the altar.

Close your eyes. Visualize yourself in varying stages of pregnancy. See your tummy expand as the months roll by. Then visualize your body in the final stage of pregnancy. Always see your face smiling radiantly. Imagine yourself going about the business of preparing for the baby's arrival, such as purchasing clothing or furniture, perhaps painting a rocking chair or toy chest, whatever it is that you intend to do in the coming months. Take your time and see everything in detail. When you feel ready, read the following prayer:

Infinite Mother, I ask for your attendance now. Please bring holy blessings with you for the infant that I carry inside my womb. Bless this child with your special love so that this babe will be healthy, strong, intelligent, and creative. Place in the tiny hands bountiful treasures for the Self of confidence, esteem, and

assurance. Bless my baby with many joys in his/her long and fruitful life, that he/she shall know abundant achievements and clever successes that will bring forth prosperity in all areas of his/her life. Most of all I ask that you bestow upon my infant compassion, empathy, and generous applications of love. Allow this wondrous creation within to share its spiritual love with one and all. I pray for the manifestation of my desires and place my trust in your infinite wisdom. Amen.

Lift the pink rose from the altar and gently remove a petal, placing the petal on top of the water in the dish. Now remove a petal and place it in the center of the white handkerchief or cloth. Continue in this manner, removing the petals one by one, floating them on the water and placing them on the cloth. Now do the same thing with the baby's breath, sprinkling the flowers on the water and into the cloth. Place two fingers into the water and then touch your forehead at the third eye. Say aloud:

Blessed am I for the wondrous creation I carry.

Lift your clothing to expose your bare belly. Place two fingers into the water again and then touch your belly. Say aloud:

Blessed is this miracle child within.

Drop your clothing. Next, enclose the petals within the cloth by gathering the fabric corners together and tying it closed with the pink ribbon and then the blue. Hold the petal bag above the incense and flame of the candles so that the smoke will purify and raise the energy of your spoken desires. Move it back and forth from one to the other and say aloud:

Blessed be this new life. May the words of all my prayers be lifted by this smoke so they may float to the ears of my ancestors for manifestation.

Place the petal bag back on the altar. Read the following declaration:

Precious Goddess, I am so very grateful to be a woman. Within me grows a seed that one day soon will blossom into a glorious flower, a flower so unique, so very special, that no other will be exactly like it. I am truly blessed to have been given this wondrous opportunity to bear this gift of life. God has not created human words adequate to express the sincere joy I feel for this miraculous event. Only the angels could speak such glorious words that would sufficiently convey my deep emotion.

Sacred Mother, I am confident in the knowledge that you will walk with me, rock with me, nurse with me, cuddle with me, and love with me as I nurture my child. Through you all things are possible. If I am weary, you will give me strength. If I am puzzled, you will give me knowledge. If I am fearful, you will still my worries. If I am doubtful, you will fill my need. I rest easy in the knowledge that you are always with me. Your wisdom is my wisdom, your love is my love, and your tenderness is my tenderness. I respectfully place myself in your loving embrace, knowing that all is right in the world and as it should be. And so it is.

Extinguish the pink candle, saying aloud:

Blessed is the love I carry inside me.

Extinguish the green candle, saying aloud:

Many blessings of prosperity are bestowed upon my child.

Extinguish the white candle, saying aloud:

My child is blessed in the purity of love.

Extinguish the blue candle, saying aloud:

My child is bathed in creative energy.

Take the petal bag outdoors. Bury it in the ground so it may be blessed and nurtured within the womb of Mother Nature. Once you have buried the petal bag, sprinkle some of the water used during the ceremony on the area. At the completion of the entire act, say these words aloud:

Blessed am I, blessed is my baby.

Return to the altar and ring the bell three times to conclude the ceremony after you bury the parcel in your yard. Proceed with the journaling exercise.

If you live in an apartment in a major city where there simply is no yard area in which to bury the parcel, save the burial time for when you can arrange to go to a park. In this particular ceremony, it is important to bury the bag of petals rather than looking for another means to fulfill the objective. There is simply no alternative method that is equally acceptable than the placement of this precious bag into the womb of Mother Earth for germination, much like the baby's seed is germinating inside of you. If the burial is to be at a later date in the park, ring the bell three times after extinguishing the candles to conclude and proceed with the journaling exercise. Save some of the water in a jar until the time when you bury the parcel. Once you have buried the rose petals in Mother Earth, sprinkle the water on the area and say these words aloud:

Blessed am I, blessed is my baby.

Journal Entries

I want this child because . . .

I receive my wisdom and strength from . . .

I pledge to always be . . .

If I should lose patience, I promise I will . . .

I will look to the Great Mother to help me when . . .

A child is God's greatest gift because . . .

Adopting Mother

Light all the candles and incense on the altar and play music that is a little livelier than you would normally use, something with a distinctive rhythm—Celtic or Native American music would do nicely. Ring the bell three times to begin the ceremony.

While standing in front of the altar, focus your eyes on the flame of the green candle. Watch it dance and sway about. Become one with the candle, allowing it to draw you in. Feel your body as it sways to the rhythm of the music. Allow yourself to be free and loose, swaying with the melody, to and fro, gently. Let your arms come out to your sides and rise above your head, delicately waving your hands about in the air. Do whatever the music wills with your body. Continue to move with the music for as long as you wish. When you tire, sit on the floor or on a chair in front of the altar.

Close your eyes. While seeing your face smiling radiantly, imagine yourself going about the business of preparing for your child's arrival, such as purchasing clothing or furniture, perhaps painting a rocking chair or toy chest, whatever it is that you intend to do in the coming months. Take your time and see everything in detail. When you feel ready, read the following prayer:

> **Infinite Mother, I ask for your attendance now. Please bring holy blessings with you for the child that I am adopting. Bless this precious soul with your special love so that this child will always be healthy, strong, intelligent, and creative. Place in his/her hands bountiful treasures for the Self of confidence, esteem, and assurance. Bless my child with many joys in his/her long and fruitful life, that he/she shall know abundant achievements and clever successes that will bring forth prosperity in all areas of its life. Most of all I ask that you bestow upon my child compassion, empathy, and generous applications of love. Allow this wondrous creation to share its spiritual love with one and all. I pray for the manifestation of my desires and place my trust in your infinite wisdom. Amen.**

Lift the pink rose from the altar and gently remove a petal, placing the petal on top of the water in the dish. Now remove a petal and place it in the center of the white handkerchief or cloth. Continue in this manner, removing the petals one by one, floating them on the water and placing them on the cloth. Now do the same thing with the baby's breath, sprinkling the flowers on the water and into the cloth. Place two fingers into the water and then touch your forehead at the third eye. Say aloud:

Blessed am I, Mother.

Enclose the petals within the cloth by gathering the fabric corners together and tying it closed with the pink ribbon and then the blue. Hold the petal bag above the incense and flame of the candles so that the smoke will purify and raise the energy of your spoken desires. Move it back and forth from one to the other and say aloud:

Blessed be this new life that will come to live with me. May the words of all my prayers be lifted by this smoke so they may float to the ears of my ancestors for manifestation.

Place the petal bag back on the altar. Read the following declaration:

Precious Goddess, I am so very grateful to be a woman. A child arrives who will one day blossom into a glorious flower, a flower so unique, so very special, that no other will be exactly like it. I am truly blessed to have been given this wondrous opportunity to be a mother. God has not created human words adequate to express the sincere joy I feel for this miraculous event. Only the angels could speak such glorious words that would convey sufficiently my deep emotion.

Sacred Mother, I am confident in the knowledge that you will walk with me, rock with me, cuddle with me, and love with me as I nurture my child. Through you all things are possible. If I am weary, you will give me strength. If I am puzzled, you will

give me knowledge. If I am fearful, you will still my worries. If I am doubtful, you will fill my need. I rest easy in the knowledge that you are always with me. Your wisdom is my wisdom, your love is my love, and your tenderness is my tenderness. I respectfully place myself in your loving embrace, knowing that all is right in the world and as it should be. And so it is.

Extinguish the pink candle, saying aloud:

Blessed is this love.

Extinguish the green candle, saying aloud:

Many blessings of prosperity are bestowed upon my child.

Extinguish the white candle, saying aloud:

My child is blessed in the purity of love.

Extinguish the blue candle, saying aloud:

My child is bathed in creative energy.

Take the petal bag outdoors. Bury it in the ground so it may be blessed and nurtured within the womb of Mother Nature. Once you have buried the petal bag, sprinkle some of the water used during the ceremony on the area. At the completion of the entire act, say these words aloud:

Blessed am I, blessed is my child.

Return to the altar and ring the bell three times to conclude the ceremony after you bury the parcel in your yard. Proceed to the journaling exercise.

If you live in an apartment in a major city where there simply is no yard area in which to bury the parcel, save the burial time for when you can arrange to go to a park. In this particular ceremony, it is important to bury the bag of petals rather than looking for another means to fulfill the objective. There is simply no alternative method that is equally acceptable than the placement of this precious bag into the womb of Mother Earth for germination, much like the baby's seed is germinating. If you will be burying it in a park, save some of the water in a jar until the time when you bury the parcel. Once you have buried the rose petals in Mother Earth, sprinkle the water on the area and say these words aloud:

Blessed am I, blessed is my child.

In the meantime, ring the bell three times to conclude the ceremony and then proceed with the journaling exercise.

Journal Entries

If I should grow cross, I will remember how blessed I am to . . .

One thing I wish to teach my child is . . .

If I had only one wish for my child, it would be . . .

The most important traits I wish to instill in my child are . . .

I will strive to always be . . .

When I need help, I can always turn to . . .

A blessed child arrives!

Affirmations for Mothers

I am blessed by Spirit

Goddess blesses me and my baby

A multitude of blessings are bestowed upon my baby

My baby is protected by God

The white light of God surrounds my baby

I am filled with mother love

The Infinite Mother blesses my child

Only goodness and blessings are attracted to my infant

The Great Mother loves my child

Everything is in divine order with my child

Healing of the Body and Heart

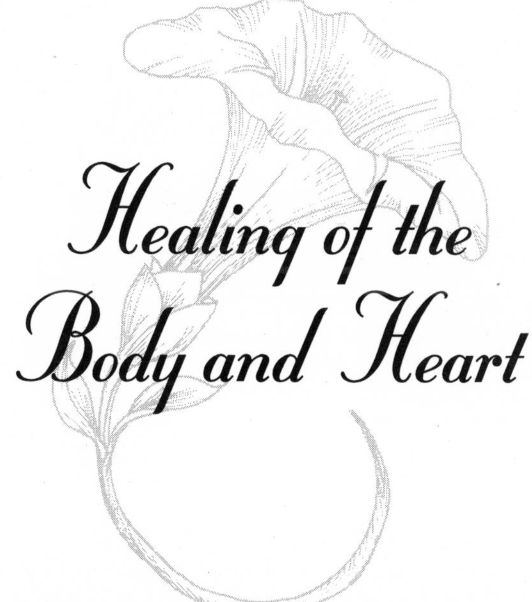

Releasing Illness

It is our desire as humans to always experience robust health. We want to be active—swimming, hiking, dancing, or simply walking around in our daily lives. It is also our constant wish to be clear-thinking individuals. However, we have all experienced periods where our bodies are not cooperating with our intentions. The latest strain of flu strikes the office and we fall victim to the attack, or some dedicated soul with a cold contaminates everyone instead of staying at home to nurse their illness. We've all been there.

The purpose of this ceremony is to get you moving in the right direction once the majority of the sickness has passed and you feel as if it is possible to return to work

and function somewhat normally. Your head may be a little stuffed up and perhaps that cough is still present but the fever is gone, along with the nausea and aches and pains. The road to recovery is here. There is no longer a risk of exposing anyone to contaminants if they are in your vicinity. If you have a serious illness, it may be beneficial to your health also to perform this ceremony.

This ceremony can be performed at any time of day or evening and nothing special is required that you wouldn't already normally have around the house. A tub is really beneficial in this particular ceremony; however, if that is not your situation, try to adjust the arrangements as best you can.

Good health surrounds me now

Burn your favorite incense in the bathroom, then light any number and color of candles you feel so led to do. Play more active music than you would normally listen to during the bathing portion, and have a spare tape with softer music available for the meditative part. The idea is to release germs while you bathe, then afterward, heal and protect to softer sounds.

Draw a hot bath using any scented bath oil of your choice. Add a little sea salt to the bath water, or regular table salt if the sea salt is not available. This is no time to go shopping for tools. The salt will help to purify the aura of those nasty germs. Have a back brush available to scrub your body. If you don't happen to have one, use a kitchen scrubby (a roundish plastic meshy item sold in groceries and discount stores for scouring Teflon pans). A loofa sponge could be used, but it should be thrown away afterward, as should the scrubby. (You may not want to part with your loofa sponge just yet, but the scrubby could easily be tossed after collecting all those sick skin cells during the ceremony.)

Ease into the hot water, allowing its liquid warmth to permeate inward. Relax into the cushion of water. Enjoy the sound of the music and the flickering candles. Experience all this for as long as you desire. Before the water cools too much, take the brush, scrubby, or loofa in hand and begin to scour away all the dead, sick skin cells clinging to your body. You will want to do this with some intensity, but do not be so brutal to your skin as to injure it.

The skin may tingle, but it shouldn't sting. Continue until you have dislodged those nasty cells from all over your body. Now drain the tub and run the shower at your normal temperature.

Shampoo your hair first, then as you rinse out the suds, let the water wash away all the exfoliated, sick skin cells from your body. Apply a conditioner to your hair. Even if you normally use a shampoo and conditioner combination or a light rinse, conditioning is a good idea at this time. It will help to restore any moisture or nutrients stripped from your hair during your illness. While the conditioner is working, lather up your body with a pleasantly scented shower gel or bar. Shave your legs if you feel the need. Then rinse your hair and body free from conditioner and soap. Take time to luxuriate in the stream of water rushing over your head and body, washing away all impurities, purifying your aura, body, mind, and spirit. As the stream of water pours over your body, know that each little droplet of water carries away impurities. Visualize any imperfections being released from your body into the water, surging down the drain in little specks. See and feel your body being purged of germs as they are carried away from you within the watery cascade. Visualize this now. When you sense that this cleansing is complete, turn off the water. At this point there are several options available. Choose whatever will make you happiest.

1. Without drying your body, pour a quarter-sized portion of almond oil into one hand, then rub your hands together. Lightly dab your hands on various parts of your wet skin to distribute the oil. Now gently rub the oil/water into your body. This will seal the moisture into your skin. Be careful not to use too much oil, though. When you have finished, softly blot any excess water from your body and towel your hair with a different towel. Put on a bathrobe or wrap up in a towel. Leave your hair damp and loose or wrap it in a towel also.
2. Towel-dry your body and hair, apply body lotion to your skin, then put on a bathrobe or wear a bath towel. Leave your hair damp and loose or wrap it in a towel.

3. Skip the above-mentioned moisturizing techniques, towel-dry your body and hair, and put on a bathrobe or wear a bath towel. Leave your hair wet and loose or wrap it in a towel. This choice is recommended for women who dislike lotions and oils or are allergic.

Change to the softer music now. Sit on a soft bath rug on the floor. If for some reason this is not an option, due to space or your physical limitations, for instance, sit on the closed commode. Close your eyes and take several very deep breaths. When exhaling, do so with intention, audibly releasing your breath in an elongated manner. Focus on the regularity of your normal breathing, in and out, in and out. Relax into the melody playing for a few moments. Now visualize yourself surrounded by the most brilliant white light energy. See it glowing and radiant all around your physical form. This is God's white light of love and protection. It is a healing light, an energy that recognizes no obstacles. It is pure love, and where there is love, only goodness can dwell. Feel the warmth of healing love that emanates from within this light energy. Know that you are bathed within the white light of God—purified, whole, healed, happy, and harmonious with all. Visualize yourself back at work, interacting with friends and family, going about your daily rounds. See yourself smiling, happy, full of energy, and very healthy. Sit for several minutes within the healing light. When you feel so inspired, take several deep breaths, move your head about, lift your shoulders, and open your eyes when you feel ready. Now get dressed!

Journal Entries

It would be healthy for my body if I . . .

Emotional stresses that may add to my illness are . . .

I will strive to eliminate them by . . .

To improve my health, what I need to eliminate is . . .

To improve my health, what I need to add is . . .

The steps I can take to prevent illness are . . .

Is there anything toxic in my environment?

You are whole and healthy!

Affirmations for Health

I am whole, healed, and happy

I am abundantly healthy

Goddess blesses me with perfect health

I am healed within the white light of God

Good health surrounds me now

I am blessed by the Goddess with robust health

I am only attracted to healthy food

Spirit walks with me on a path of health

Where there is love there is healing

I dwell within the healing bubble of white light

Forgiving Mother

It is wonderful when women can be friends with their mothers. I feel those who have a close relationship with their primary teacher of womanhood are truly blessed. Unfortunately, this was not my experience. Like many women, my mother and I were challenged to be agreeable with each other when I was a child and as an adult. Perhaps you will identify with my story.

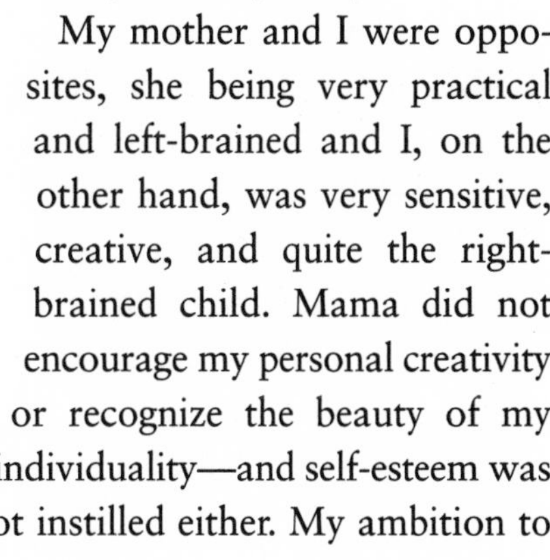

My mother and I were opposites, she being very practical and left-brained and I, on the other hand, was very sensitive, creative, and quite the right-brained child. Mama did not encourage my personal creativity or recognize the beauty of my individuality—and self-esteem was not instilled either. My ambition to be an actress was strongly discouraged, and I was dissuaded from attending college. Mama thought I would be better suited to seek employment in the clerical field after high school, as she had. Even though both of my parents were very proud of my natural artistic ability, neither encouraged me to attend art school because it wasn't practical. I am sure my parents, especially my mother, thought they were doing the right thing. What was good for my mother would be good for me.

I am a whole, happy woman

Today parents are told to instill self-confidence in their female children and to encourage their girls to believe that they can do anything they set their minds to. Females are entering military academies where women once were not allowed to attend. It would have been unheard of to even think such a thing was possible when I was growing up. Instead, the preferred idea was to train young girls to be ladies. Consequently, my mother drilled into my head the importance of behaving like a lady and what was the most appropriate to wear. Ironically, she never taught me how to cook, yet stressed the importance of what other people thought because she didn't want the neighbors to talk. Looking back, I can only surmise she was following the examples set by *her* mother.

When I was nineteen and employed by the government as a clerk typist, just like my mother, I decided I wanted to move out on my own. I so desperately wanted to sail on my butterfly wings into independence. I was told that I could leave home, however, I couldn't take my car with me. The vehicle was titled in my father's name and mine. Because I lived in the metropolitan area of Washington, D.C., I needed a car desperately. Public transportation was not an option for me. So I remained home with my parents until I figured out a way to solve my problem—I married the first guy who asked. That marriage ended two years later. Finally, at the age of twenty-two, I had the freedom I had been trying so hard to obtain.

Looking back on that issue, I realize now that my parents were trying to protect their only child. I have to admit that I was not mature for my age. I was ill-equipped to handle responsibility, so I could have been a disaster waiting to happen. But since I had not been given any opportunities to be independent, I held a belly full of resentment, especially toward my mother.

As an adult, I wanted my mother to be proud of me and respect my choices. But we just weren't on the same wavelength. My early childhood treatment and the continued lack of respect hurt my spirit.

After my father passed away, my mother moved to a Florida town not too far from my then-husband and me and, graciously, not too close either. For the better part of the next three years, we were friends. The only thing that had changed within our lives was that she was now a widow. Perhaps she felt vulnerable and saw me as some form of security. I don't know. Whatever it was, we actually enjoyed spending time with each other. Then she was diagnosed with stomach cancer. Although the cancer did not return after surgery, eventually she was forced by her declining health to move in with me. Suddenly, the roles changed. I was the mother and she was the child. As her weakness progressed, she became very angry when I took the controlling role over her life, since she was incapable physically of managing anything. These were very stressful times for both of us.

My mother passed to spirit December 14, 1989. Just hours before her spirit left her body, I was fortunate to be able to tell my mother that I loved her. This was important to me because I wanted us to part on relatively good terms. She was incapable of acknowledging my endearments since she was not fully cognizant at the time. But I knew on some level of her being that she heard me. Her soul heard me, and her spirit responded in kind. I had always loved my mother, I just didn't particularly like her sometimes. And there was no doubt in my mind that my mother (and father) always loved me, perhaps too much.

Unfortunately, I continued to harbor resentment after her passing regarding her treatment of me, and other physical characteristics that were a result of my childhood stresses did not disappear either, such as my shortness of breath. Every once in awhile I would be struck with the desire to relieve myself of this animosity. I would journal and meditate, counsel myself, and perhaps speak to friends. When I thought everything was okay inside, I would drop this action. Down the road, inevitably, something would occur that would trigger those old emotions, letting me know that I really hadn't put all the "stuff" behind me as I had convinced myself I had.

The imbalance I experienced with my mother is not unique to me. I know many of you who are reading this book are sitting in the same corner as me, and some of you have even worse stories to tell. If you are one who has not released your old baggage from your younger years, you may wish to purge some "junk" by doing a little emotional housecleaning. That is why I felt it was necessary to provide a ceremony for understanding and forgiveness of mother. It does not serve our spiritual growth to hang on to negative emotions regarding our parents. Actually, this ceremony could be used when there is an issue with the father also, if someone felt so inclined to perform it that way.

It was difficult to write a ceremony about forgiving a mother's perceived transgressions since at the time I hadn't grown past that issue myself. My personal desire, also, was to be standing where I was trying to lead the reader. But I found comfort in the fact that I didn't have to do this alone. All women are our sisters. Together, those who have walked this path can create a happier, whole woman. We may shed some tears on this journey, but they will certainly be tears that cleanse. I finally was inspired with a ceremony that worked for me and for several friends of mine. It is my hope that this ceremony will heal your spirit, as it did mine.

There cannot be a recommended time or a more appropriate period in one's life in which to perform this ceremony. We all will come to this at our own pace. I would at least like to make the suggestion that when you feel so led, plan the ritual during the waning moon, when the moon goes from full to dark. This is the time for release, banishment, and reversal. I do not feel that the hour is important, but I would strongly advise no matter what the time of day, be sober. Read the entire ceremony before attempting the performance.

The tools you will need for this ceremony of healing are as follows:

1. An incense for harmony and cleansing, such as cedar or lavender.
2. Choose a green candle for balance and healing; pink for love; white for cleansing; blue for peace; and purple for spiritual wisdom.
3. Agate, amethyst, aventurine, citrine, jasper, jet, malachite, moonstone, pearl, rock crystal, rose quartz, snow quartz, sapphire, and tourmaline. Use all the stones or as many as you have in your possession. Wear them or place them on the altar.

4. A dish of water.
5. A dish of salt.
6. A picture of your mother.
7. A sacred object, if desired.
8. A small bell.
9. A journal and a pen.
10. A box of tissues.
11. An object of your choice on which to focus negative feelings. This should be something that can be discarded, such as a rock, paper towel, crumpled paper, etc.

Directly before the performance of the ceremony, spend some time cleansing your body. Draw a warm bath, if possible, using rose-scented bath oil. Sprinkle some sea salt into the bath water if you wish to boost the cleansing process. If you have a shower, use a rose-scented bath gel or bar and gently rub salt into the lather. While you bathe, have pink and green candles lit and soft music playing. Lavender incense would be nice. After the bath is complete, wear a loose-fitting garment in a natural fabric in the shade of blue or white.

Light all the candles and incense on the altar. Play soft music. Ring the bell three times to begin the ceremony. Take the incense in hand and direct it in figure eights in front of your body, first down low and then raising it until you reach the top of your head. While continually making the motion of figure eights, walk into the smoke so that it blends with your aura. Turn around and walk into it again. Return the incense to the altar. Standing in front of the altar, raise your arms above your head and stretch both hands upward. Stretch! Stretch one arm, then the other. Now both again. Bring both arms back down together until they touch your sides and, as you do so, lower your chin to your chest. Stretch the neck forward, then to the right, backward, to the left, and forward again. Raise your head to a normal position. Let your body fall forward from the waist until your hands come to rest on the floor or as close as flexibility will allow. Hang for a minute, visualizing any kinks or tension flowing down from your body exiting through your hands or feet.

When you feel ready, either bend your legs to sit on the floor or back into a chair positioned in front of the altar. Take a deep breath. Take another deep breath and exhale audibly through your mouth.

During the first portion of this ceremony you will be asking yourself some questions about your mother. The idea is to try to release any preconceived opinions about her for the purpose of seeing the real person. Take time with each question, contemplating with closed eyes on the answers that you give. Let your imagination run, perhaps seeing scenarios play out in your mind from when you were a child. Then write in your journal the realizations that come to you as you deal with each question. A new understanding about your mother will be your gift. Begin the process of healing by saying aloud the following prayer:

> **Guardian Spirit, I pray for understanding of my mother. Let my heart be an open vessel so that I may receive your wisdom. Allow me to know this woman who delivered me into this world. Help me to understand her beliefs, dreams, and what was important to her and why. I seek only truth because I know through knowledge I will receive release from this anguish that has haunted me. Please, dear Spirit, assist me in this endeavor so that I may also come to understand myself more fully, thereby growing beyond this obstacle that has blocked my spiritual evolution. Amen.**

In your journal, ask yourself these questions:

> **What kind of a person was my mother when I was a child?**

> **What was important to her?**

> **Did she have aspirations?**

Were all her desires realized eventually or did she feel cheated?

Was she happy?

What kind of a relationship did my parents have when I was young? Did they love each other?

What was her relationship with her mother (my grandmother)?

Did my grandmother discipline my mother the same way my mother punished me as a child? (Did grandma use a belt or lock my mother in a closet, for instance?)

What kind of mother would I imagine my grandmother to have been, given the knowledge I have?

Could there have been reasons why my mother treated me as she did due to conditioning from her childhood or her relationship with my father? If so, what?

Was my mother mentally ill or a substance abuser?

What possible explanation can I give for her behavior?

When you are finished, focus your attention on the object you have selected to receive your negative emotions. Hold it in your hand and read the following declaration:

> **Beloved Mother, ancestral mothers, Spirit, and spiritual guardians, attend me now that I may find peace within. My heart has been saddened for far too long, my emotions bruised, my thoughts askew. The time is now to banish these old, useless feelings, these well-worn and torn emotions. I have carried this burden long enough and I will not labor under its heaviness anymore. I rid myself of this self-abuse, these destructive patterns that harm only me. This is not my load to carry. This is not my baggage. These abusive acts were cast upon me due to another's misguided intentions. It was a sorry day that I accepted the words hurled at me, believing them to be true. It was a mournful day I received the physical blow, trusting that I was deserving. NO! I shout NO! This is not mine to bear. NO! I shout again, these words are not truth. NO! I shout again, this harm is not deserved. Into this object I hurl my ugly thoughts, deeply wounded emotions, and any bitterness as a result of my childhood. This wretched horror that has tormented me can no longer be contained. I cast it upon this object, never to be returned to me, never to be revisited.**

Focus your eyes on your object of negativity, and direct all your animosity into it. Feel it flow from you into it. Visualize particles traveling from you to the rock, paper towel, crumpled paper, or whatever you have chosen. See these floating particles as dark items lodging in the object. Audibly send negativity into your chosen object. Scream sentences at it. Roar as loud as you can, all the while feeling that you are spewing the total of your anger, animosity, and ugliness into the object of negativity. When you feel there is no more venom remaining and you are emotionally spent, discard this negativity-laden object. Throw it out the door. Flush it down the toilet. Fling it down the trash chute. Put it in among the deposits within the kitty litter bag sitting in the garbage can outside. Get rid of it!

Once you have disposed of your object of negativity, read aloud the following declaration:

> **Let all the gods in heaven, all the angels present, and all that is holy hear my words: I am a child of God. I am beautiful. I am whole. I am healed. God loves me dearly in all ways and always. These are words of truth. These are truly words of love.**
>
> **I am a physical manifestation of God. Should doubts enter my thinking, I need only to remind myself of this fact. I am a child of God. Should uncertainty invade my life, I need only to remember that Goddess loves me now and forever. This is truth.**
>
> **I am filled with the limitless understanding of Spirit. The new pathway on which I have begun is paved with love from the angelic kingdom, granting me a new appreciation of my mother. I am capable of feeling sympathy and compassion, for I now better understand the path she has walked. I see clearly her difficulties, for she was a victim of her circumstance as surely as I was. Had things been different in her life, so would mine have been. I must ask myself, given the choice, would my mother have chosen to behave as she did? Would she have deliberately [illegible] he had known the consequences I would suffer? No. [illegible] is simply, no. My mother did the very best she could [illegible] he had to work with, considering her understanding [illegible]. My heart is filled with God's love and only that [illegible] will be reflected upon my mother from now on. [illegible] Spirit, for this experience. I am growing.**

[illegible] sense of relief and release, providing you earnestly per[illegible] ny with the intention of dismissing all animosity. Now, [illegible] ing journal entry.

Journal Entries

Three things I am grateful to my mother for teaching me are . . .

What I most admire about my mother is . . .

My mother showed me love by . . .

One way I can move forward is to . . .

I am beautiful because . . .

I am most talented in these areas . . .

I am stronger because . . .

Following up with affirmations placed in various places around your house will also boost the benefits from this ceremony. In the future, if you happen to feel twinges of negative emotions poking at you or a lack of self-esteem, I suggest that you read your journal exercise and the section of the ceremony where you gave answers to questions about your mother. This should help to dislodge any negative emotion still lingering in the recesses of your heart that escaped your original emotional housecleaning.

Extinguish the blue candle, saying aloud:

Spirit encloses me within a peace-filled bubble now.

Extinguish the purple candle, saying aloud:

I am grateful for this newfound wisdom.

Extinguish the pink candle, saying aloud:

Only love fills my forgiving heart.

Extinguish the white candle, saying aloud:

Thank you, Goddess, for cleansing my emotions.

Extinguish the green candle, saying aloud:

I am whole, healed, and balanced now.

Ring the bell three times to conclude the ceremony.

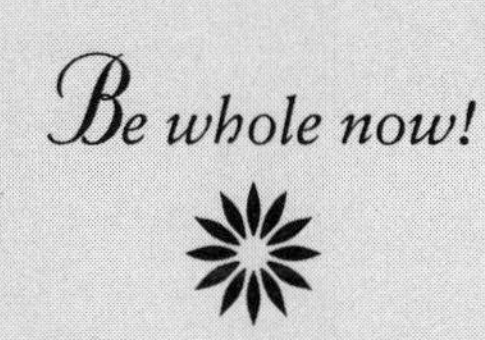

Affirmations for Forgiving Mother

I am a whole, happy woman

Goddess loves me always and in all ways

I am a child of God

Goddess blesses me with new understanding and compassion

The stones on my path are merely stepping stones

I am filled with the limitless understanding of Spirit

I love my mother

I forgive my mother

God bless my mother

I am grateful for the lessons given to me

Pathways In Our Lives

Return to Romance

No one can question that motherhood is a blessing. Being part of the creation of another human being, the vessel through which a soul is given entry into this world, is truly a blessed gift. However, with motherhood comes the willing sacrifice of personal desires, private time, and spiritual moments, placing the needs of our children first. When little ones are very young, everything must be scheduled around nap time, feedings, and play time. Once they become more mature, a mother's time often is spent depositing one child or another at various activities, such as school, baseball practice, ballet class, and piano or karate lessons. In the teen years they present us with many growth

opportunities as they insist they know what is best for them and attempt to stretch their independence as far as we are willing to allow. Eventually, as young adults, they expand their horizons through college, careers, and marriage, and time becomes more abundant for both parents. This is when a personal life can begin again for mother—another blessing!

If you are involved in a loving partnership and the last child has flown out of the nest, now life can return to romance. Remember the early days in your relationship? Reflect back on those times before the patter of little feet resounded throughout the house. Your movements were probably more spontaneous and uninhibited. Uninterrupted lovemaking was normal and could be enjoyed at any hour of the day or night. An evening out was easy to plan without having to consider the availability of a sitter. You could create special dinners without regard to children's tastes and nutritional requirements. Now you can again.

Life is full of change. This is one change you can learn to enjoy! If you have a fireplace, how about sipping champagne and nibbling cheese cubes and sliced apples by firelight? (Be sure to have large pillows around in anticipation that something else will develop!) Or if you have a pool, a moonlight swim is the perfect, sensual adventure to ignite passion. Quiet, romantic candlelight dinners that were a thing of the past can now become a weekly event, as well as trips to the movies or theater. Weekend journeys to country inns after a day of antique shopping, or camping outdoors and hiking in the woods, are wonderful getaways for couples. The options are too numerous to mention. Use your imagination! Seek those precious moments together and spark the romance once again.

Perhaps you are single now and, with the children gone, the house seems empty. Consider this: a full cup of water cannot accept more liquid, and what is made empty has room to be filled anew. This is the perfect time for personal growth and new beginnings. Now you have a chance to seek those grand adventures and exciting happenings that you may not have experienced before or recently. Time will now allow you to take that Spanish course or meditation class. Weekends do not have to be spent catching up on the housework and laundry anymore. They can become breaks in which you challenge yourself with rock climbing excursions, biking through the countryside, or enjoying restful periods sunning on the beach. Why not start that home business that has been burning in your brain? Begin by converting one bedroom into an office or workroom. Perhaps this is a good time to unfold your easel and open that box of oil paints now that you have room for a studio. This is your opportunity to investigate something new and untried, an exploration of life and Self.

Whether you are cohabiting, married, or single, you can choose to view what some people call the empty nest as a natural circumstance that will allow time for personal growth. It's an opportunity to rediscover or get better acquainted with your Self and romance yourself. You are the priority for a change—my goodness, aren't you worth it?

Creative energy fills my days

Two friends of mine were experiencing the empty nest syndrome at the same time. Marie had never pursued a career all through her marriage and child-rearing days. When all three children were away at college, suddenly she had too much time on her hands. Marie became lazy, unable to manage her daily routine. She spent her days in front of the TV while her house was in need of a good scrubbing and vacuuming. Marie longed for her husband to come home from work so they could go out to a movie or some other form of entertainment.

The other friend, Susan, found herself divorced while both her children were married and living at a distance. She began hitting the clubs at night. Pretty soon Susan had a new live-in boyfriend, fourteen years her junior, with two children under the age of six in his custody. She began baking cookies for the kids, buying them clothes, and bubbling all around the house in her renewed role as Mom. She was in her glory.

The problem with both of these women was that they had never created a personal life for themselves. They only had seen their role as Mother. This is a very sad state of affairs for any woman to have created for herself. But there is some good news.

Marie performed the following ceremony, purchased books relating to self-esteem, took two business courses at a community college, and is in the process of redesigning one of the bedrooms in their house into an office. With assistance from her husband, Marie plans to start a service-related business that she can manage from her home. I'm very proud of her. And, by the way—as busy as she is now, Marie always has a clean house.

Susan, on the other hand, still doesn't understand that she needs to get a life. She feels that men are the answer to all her problems, especially if they come with children in hand. Susan thrives on the drama of the situations she creates and continually complains to me about the same problems. Nothing ever changes. I don't have any patience left for her, but I send my blessings for her evolution.

Please read the entire ceremony prior to attempting the performance. The best time would be during the waxing moon. This is the period after the new moon to the full moon, which is intended to bring upliftment, improvement, and increase. Any ceremony performed exactly on the full moon brings with it the most energy.

Before you do the ritual it is important to bathe. This purifying process is necessary in order to wash away any barriers so that you will be a clear channel for spiritual energy. A bubble bath with a deliciously scented bath oil would be perfect. If you do not have a tub, use a scented bath soap or gel. I would suggest vanilla for the fragrance. Play soft music and have candles burning. When you have completed your relaxing cleanse, wear a loose-fitting garment in a natural fabric that is colored white, blue, or pink. It is especially important to be of a sober mind. You do not want to inhibit your spiritual work by contaminating yourself with intoxicants.

The tools you will need are as follows:

1. The incense of your choice for balance and harmony, like rose, jasmine, lilac, or patchouli.
2. A green candle for balance; blue for serenity; orange for putting things in motion; and pink for self-love.
3. Citrine, aventurine, amethyst, fluorite, garnet, malachite, moonstone, snow quartz, rose quartz, and tourmaline. Use all the stones or as many as you have in your possession. Wear them or place them on the altar.
4. A dish of water.

5. A dish of salt.
6. A sacred object.
7. A journal and a pen.
8. A small bell.

After preparing yourself properly, play soft music and light the candles and incense on the altar. Fan the smoke of the incense toward your body with your hands so that you may be cleansed by the smoke. Sit on the floor or on a chair in front of the altar, close your eyes, and take a few deep breaths, filling your lungs with the gift of life. Now focus on your regular breathing—in and out, in and out.

Visualize yourself surrounded by a beautiful ball of white light. This light energy is from your spiritual source. Envision this light totally encompassing your physical form, enfolding you within the loving embrace of spiritual comfort. Mentally send white light energy into all the rooms of your dwelling, seeing the light fill each room with a brilliant radiance. Take your time. All these spaces within your home are sacred because you live there. As you mentally journey through each room, reflect on special moments that have taken place in any of these areas. Speak to yourself silently as you visit, saying phrases like, *Light fills my home. Love fills my abode. God and Goddess dwell within my sanctuary.*

Draw your attention to your heart center. Breathe in and out, focusing on this area of your being. Let it become warm and allow it to expand. Open your heart chakra and feel all the love you have within. Know that the love you carry will always exist. Realize that this love dwells within your home and will remain forever. Open your eyes and read this prayer aloud:

> **My dear Spiritual Creator, I thank you for my continuing opportunity for growth. As I reflect gently back on motherhood, I know I accomplished everything to the best of my ability, given my understanding at that time. We all grew from the myriad of experiences we encountered. I am proud of myself. I am proud of my child/children. Now the time has come for each of us to**

stand on our own, forever united spiritually although physically separate. The window of opportunity shines brightly for all of us. I look to our future with anticipation sparkling in my eyes. I welcome my new personal fulfillment with an open heart.

The rooms in my home are forever filled with love and memories. As I traveled mentally through each room, radiating white light energy, I opened the doors to my soul so that I might attract further blessings. My path is clear and unobstructed. I stand ready and eager to receive all the creative energy that is being channeled my way. Each day brings forth more glorious events and continued successes. I am forever grateful for the opportunity at this time in my life for expansion. Only the highest and best awaits me. Spirit blesses me each day with the realization that I am a creative being filled with light, love, and abundant choices. Ideas pour like a beautiful waterfall into my mind, where they are nurtured into exciting outcomes. I only need to extend my hands to receive what is already mine by divine right.

I seek to rediscover myself spiritually. I reach out with faith to the angelic presence that is forever in my life. I am open to receiving spiritual guidance and will anticipate revealing scenarios manifesting in my life for my highest growth. My willing spirit stands ready to venture onto new roadways that will lead me to a deeper attunement with my higher Self and Creator. I am evolving into a more fulfilled, intuitive being who understands the goodness one receives by blessing each circumstance. My heart is eager as I look ahead to my new life. I behold this to be a glorious day! I am fruitful now! Amen.

Complete the following journal exercise.

Journal Entries

What are my three best personality traits?

What are my talents?

What are my pleasures in life?

How can I use any of the above to my advantage in the future?

This experience has taught me that . . .

In my happiness, I can attract prosperity in all forms by . . .

Ring the bell three times to conclude the ceremony.

Affirmations for Personal Growth

Abundance is my constant companion

Creative energy fills my days

Goddess blesses each endeavor

Spirit watches over all my new aspirations

I hear the voice of my ancestors directing me

My heart is filled with love for myself

I am important

I am prosperous in every part of my life now

Spirit guides many happy adventures to my door now

Goddess holds me within her loving embrace

The Sisterhood of Menopause

Currently among my circle of women friends one of the most frequently discussed topics is hot flashes (or "power surges," as one of them prefers to call this heated experience). It appears, at least within my group, that this particular facet of womanhood is viewed either as an unwelcome perplexity or with awe and wonder.

I have read articles about how some women struggle with the process of menopause. One single woman friend is having a difficult time adjusting, confessing a fear of growing older without a mate. On the other hand, a student of mine is fascinated by the amount of heat her body exudes. Once her hot flashes have subsided, for several minutes

thereafter her clothes feel as if they have just been freshly ironed. She simply marvels at the wonders her body creates, and sports a bumper sticker on her vehicle extolling power surges.

Hot flashes (or power surges), anxiety attacks, and emotional ups and downs are some of the occurrences shared by women who are traveling on the menopause road. Menopause is a common experience that manifests in all women's lives, either naturally or surgically. It is but another change in life that brings on a new beginning. The common theme throughout this book has been that when one door closes another one opens so that we may receive something better. Menopause is no different.

I'm not going to pretend that the performance of a ceremony will make hot flashes disappear or mood swings subside. I can honestly state that it will give you a positive perspective while you are going through this change in your life. Thinking negative thoughts and cursing every human being for your condition will not rectify anything. Focusing on the positive will assist in your emotional well-being, which is a large part of the battle.

We should all find comfort in the realization that we do not have to go through this alone.

The first Tuesday of each month, my local health food store has a 20 percent off day. The place is jammed with people purchasing vitamins, herbs, and food. One particular Tuesday I was searching for herbs to diminish my night sweats and help me sleep. In the herb aisle one women was asking another about natural remedies for hot flashes. Apparently the lady had some experience with controlling the unpredictable surges of heat. A third women asked if she could join the conversation, and at that point I started adding my two cents. Pretty soon the aisle had six women exchanging information about hot flashes and how to sleep better. I found this experience amusing and enlightening—like I was a part of an elite group.

Ladies, we are not alone on this journey! Gathering with friends and sharing our experiences brings a great deal of comfort. Personally, I appreciate the knowledge that what I am experiencing is normal. This is simply another stepping stone on the walk of life, and only a temporary one at that.

Women belong to a unique sorority, and when we graduate from menopause, we will all be wiser and stronger for the experience. Let us be open to increased self-expression through our ever-developing spirituality and a newfound freedom for our souls! Wisdom walks with us now. A common term for a woman who has entered menopause is wise woman. Let us wear that badge with the pride and dignity it deserves.

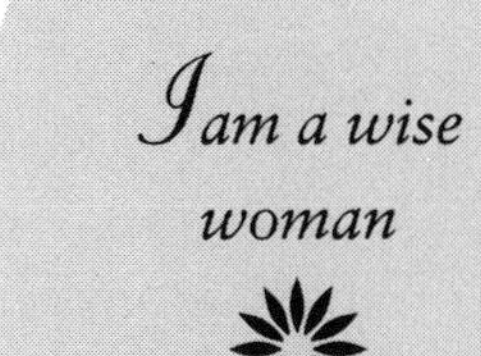

It would be best to perform this ceremony after it has been determined that you have completed the process and have entered menopause. Please read everything before starting. The following items will be needed for this ceremony:

1. Choose an incense for balance and peace, such as rose or lavender, for the altar.
2. Select a green candle for balance and renewal; yellow for change; orange for putting things in motion; and purple for inspiration and spiritual wisdom.
3. Amethyst, citrine, diamond, fluorite, garnet, lapis, malachite, moonstone, pearl, snow quartz, and tourmaline. Use all the stones or as many as you have in your possession. Wear them or place them on the altar.
4. A dish of water.
5. A dish of salt.
6. A sacred object.
7. A gentle bell.
8. A journal and a pen.

I would suggest the best time to perform this ceremony is early morning, when everything is waking to the dawn of a new day. Begin by preparing yourself. Light the bathroom with purple and white candles—as many as you like. Burn an incense for peace and purification, such as lavender, cedar, or jasmine, in the bathroom. Use a bath oil or shower gel in your favorite scent. After you have bathed, white or purple clothing is necessary so you may present yourself in the most spiritual manner. Wear and/or place some of the stones on the altar, light the incense, and play soft music. Do not light the candles yet.

Begin by ringing the bell three times and then remain standing, facing the front of the altar. Fan the smoke from the incense with your hands so it blends with your aura. Now allow the music to penetrate your body. Let it fill your soul and move your body rhythmically. Release, let go, flow, sway. Touch your body wherever you are comfortable. This is your body; it belongs to you. Place your hands on your hips, your tummy, your shoulders, your face, and elsewhere. Allow your hands to be guided by Spirit. Feel your skin, the fabric under your hands, the texture of your hair. This is you, the physical, the human manifestation of a Goddess creation. You are magnificent in your physical glory. Love this perfection for the wonder it truly is. Marvel at the beauty of the physical form. (Force yourself to ignore any extra poundage or self-perceived imperfections. This is not about vanity.) Let your arms float outward and upward as you enjoy how the music plays with you. Take several deep breaths, stretching your arms overhead as you inhale and letting them slowly fall again to your sides as you exhale. Sit on the floor or a chair in front of the altar and close your eyes.

Draw your attention to your breathing—in and out, in and out, slowly, gently. See and feel a brilliant white light form at the center of your chest, sparkling radiantly, warming the chest area. Take notice as the white light increases in size until you are completely engulfed in the beautiful energy of this light. Bask within the radiance for a moment. Now contemplate on your womanliness, what qualities and interests separate you from men. Reflect on those special characteristics that uniquely spell out WOMAN, defining you as the wondrous creature you are. Enjoy this reflective period; be proud of your gender. Take as long as you need. When you are finished, stand up and light the yellow candle. Begin to read the following declaration, pausing to absorb the message when you feel inspired to do so.

> **Precious Mother, I stand ready to be guided on my new journey. My world is changing, as it has many times before. I trust in the belief that what lies ahead is for my highest and best good, as has always been my experience. Goddess has unceasingly held my hand through difficult periods and focused light on the path**

ahead so my feet could easily follow. I accept the changes I have already experienced and welcome those that are just ahead. With change comes opportunity, growth, enlightenment, expansion, and fulfillment. As I light the green candle (light the candle), I know in the recesses of my heart that my life is in perfect balance. Just as when winter ceases to grace the Earth with snow and spring abundantly appears everywhere in colorful floral displays, I, too, am enfolded within cyclical harmony. Within this fond embrace, I know everything is in divine order. Peace and harmony swell within my heart, bringing a newfound balance to my existence. The stones on my path turn to pearls once I have left them behind, and I am wiser for the exchange. I look forward to all those exquisite experiences that will further my spiritual development, bringing me utter tranquillity.

(Light the orange candle.) Many avenues beckon to me for attention. I am a multifaceted being who is capable of more successes and greater achievements than I have experienced thus far on my personal Earth journey. I remain open to the delicate urgings that speak quietly to me during my silent moments. Spirit prompts me to challenge my abilities and stretch my boundaries into broader horizons. My will is insurmountable. I am the lioness, strong and clever. I am the owl, wise and true. My best is yet to come because I have only just begun.

I light the purple candle (light the candle) in recognition of my spirituality. From the day of my birth, my spiritual flame has been nurtured through experience until it has blazed into this inferno of light energy residing within. It reminds me of its presence whenever I feel my heart expand with love. I am the dove, loving and peaceful. I am the doe, sweet and gentle. My spiritual Self has manifested in ways only time could provide. Like a diamond, it shines forth after years of cultivation. I will shine my

light on those who may benefit from my wisdom. I have much to share. Behind me is a score of happenings that have produced a basketful of knowledge. I have so much more to give at this time in my life than I did many years ago. Thank you, Goddess, for bestowing upon me all these wondrous blessings. I am forever grateful for all my experiences, for they have brought me to this pinnacle of spirituality. I am worthy of the name wise woman. Many have gone before me and many more shall follow my steps within the light. I am a beacon of hope, accomplishment, courage, serenity, strength, dignity, perseverance, and faith, proof that everything—everything—somehow works out for the best. Thank you, Spirit, for this new day and all the ones that will follow. I step forward now renewed and whole within my being.

Now, complete the following journal exercise.

Journal Entries

Where do I want my next journey to begin?

Who would I include in this adventure?

What do I want to accomplish?

Why am I more capable now of completing this than I was before?

If given the opportunity, what special knowledge would I share with other women?

I am empowered because . . .

I am a wise woman because . . .

I display my peaceful warrior side when . . .

When you are done, snuff out the candles.
Extinguish the purple candle, saying:

I am a wise woman.

Extinguish the orange candle, saying:

I am the Goddess in action.

Extinguish the green candle, saying:

I am filled with peace and harmony.

Extinguish the yellow candle, saying:

Opportunity knocks loudly at my door.

Your best is yet to come because you have only just begun!

Ring the bell three times to conclude the ceremony. Creating a treasure map would be beneficial to your well-being at this time. Allow inspiration to guide your design, perhaps being more outrageous than you have dared to be in the past. Hey, you are a wise woman—go for it!

Affirmations for Menopause

I am filled with wisdom

I am a powerful woman

Goddess blesses me with infinite wisdom

Spirit guides my spiritual path

I am filled with peace and harmony

I am the wise owl

The Heavenly Mother walks with me now

I walk within Goddess' light

The ancestral mothers guide my path

I am the daughter of (name), who is the daughter of (name),
and we form a powerful trinity

Homeward Bound

My father used to say, "The only thing I have to do is die and pay taxes." I am sure this is a familiar phrase and perhaps a commonly held sentiment. Everyone who is born into this world eventually will depart from it. A significant part of life is death. According to *Funk and Wagnalls Standard Dictionary*, the definition of the word "death" is the extinction of something, the cessation of physical life. As a minister I do not believe or teach that the death of the body means a finality or ending of life, because we are so much more than a mere physical body. We are also a soul and a spirit. The physical person may cease to exist but the spiritual entity is still very much alive.

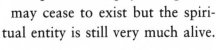

That personality, those opinions and characteristics—they still exist. Science has proven that energy never dies. We are energy. We live. We transform. We survive. We just don't do it on Earth any longer.

When referring to death, I prefer to use the word "passed" or phrases such as "passed away," "passed over," or "passed on." I also use phrases like "he's in spirit" or "she is on the spirit side of life." To me this is a more accurate description of a life whose energy has transformed, minus the negative connotations associated with other commonly used words.

Energy never dies

While our loved ones and friends are still on the Earth plane, we should show our appreciation and express our love for them. I am reminded of some advice my widowed mother gave to her sister when she and her husband were visiting my mother one winter in Florida. During the week the couple was staying at the riverside condominium my mother owned, my Aunt Lil bickered and criticized Uncle Mason and showed little, if any, patience for his shortcomings. Apparently, that was a normal behavior pattern. Finally, my mother reached the point where she could no longer tolerate her sister's sharp tone. So she sat in private with my aunt and expressed her concern. She told Lil how fortunate she was to have Mason for a husband, reminding Lil that she, herself, was widowed and how much she missed her deceased husband. My mother further admonished my aunt to change her attitude to one of appreciation, because in the beat of a heart, it could all disappear and her life could change radically. After their little chat, Aunt Lil became much more accommodating and agreeable with Mason.

On a more personal note, the mother of my first husband and I were sharing some time together in her big country kitchen. I was complaining about her son's excessively loud snoring, to which she responded, "Be thankful when you hear Bill snore in the middle of the night. After my husband died, during the wee hours of the night as I laid there all alone in bed, I missed hearing his snoring." Coming from a women who had lost her husband, that statement had a great impact on me. I never minded the snoring after that conversation and I certainly did not forget the advice.

While they are sharing your Earth journey, make sure everyone who holds an important place in your life knows you love, cherish, and value them. People need to know they are special in your eyes. We never know when something unfortunate may occur without warning, leaving us to wish we had said "I love you" before they went to work, hugged before we left town, or written an adoring letter, just because. Since closure is so important to people, I would like to encourage you to express yourself now so there will never be a time when you feel *I wish I had . . .*

If I could take back . . .

If I could just have one more minute to say I love you.

My sympathies are strongest for the people who are left behind. The one who has passed over to the other side of life is in a far better state of being and, in most cases, happy to be there. The family members and friends who remain on their Earth journey are left to cope with the loss of their loved one. They deserve comfort and heaping measures of sympathy and compassion from those of us in a position to aid in their recovery. This chapter has been created for the times when you or someone you know is grieving the loss of a special person. The ceremonies contained herein may be shared with anyone you know who needs release from grief.

Some of you may be in a position now where you have regrets. The ceremony that follows is intended to help bring closure for you.

Closure of the Past

The purpose of this ceremony is to provide a vehicle through which one may release any guilt or regrets felt after the passing of a friend or loved one. This is the perfect ceremony for those individuals who feel there is more to be said and require some form of closure in order to venture forth in their lives. As usual, please read the entire ceremony before the performance.

The following tools will be needed to perform either ceremony:

1. Choose an incense for balance, peace, and love, like rose or jasmine.

2. Select a green candle for balance; blue for tranquillity; pink for love; and purple for spirituality.
3. Amethyst, aventurine, diamond, lapis, malachite, moonstone, pearl, rock crystal, rose quartz, and tourmaline. Use all the stones or as many as you have in your possession. Wear them or place them on the altar.
4. A sacred object is strongly recommended for this ceremony, either worn or placed on the altar.
5. A dish of water.
6. A dish of salt.
7. A gentle bell.
8. A box of tissues.
9. A picture of the person, if available.
10. Soft music, especially something enjoyed by this person.
11. A journal and a pen.

As is customary, bathe prior to the ceremony and be sober. A rose bath oil, soap, or gel would be most desirable. Pink candles burning during the bathing process would be very nice, along with soft music. For this particular ritual, I would suggest wearing a white or purple loose-fitting garment in a natural fabric.

After you have prepared yourself appropriately, light the incense, play soft music, then ring the bell three times. Do not light the candles yet. Begin by standing in front of the altar and inhaling deeply, filling your lungs and releasing the air slowly. With your hands, fan the smoke from the incense toward your body so it blends with your aura. Light the green candle and say:

I light the green candle as a symbol for balance and ask that harmony enter into my daily life once again.

Light the blue candle and say the following:

With the lighting of the blue candle, I evoke tranquillity and peace into all areas of my life.

Light the pink candle and smile. Be conscious of your heart center and say:

As I light this pink candle, I feel love for my Self and for (name).

Light the purple candle and say:

By lighting this candle I am summoning spiritual purity to attend this ceremony.

Sit on the floor or in a chair in front of the altar and close your eyes. Take several deep breaths. Raise your shoulders, then deliberately drop them heavily, exhaling at the same time. Do this several more times. Tense the feet and ankles, then release. Continue up your legs, tightening and releasing the muscles. Do the same with the stomach muscles and then your arms. Turn your head side to side, backward and forward. Take a deep breath and exhale slowly.

Bring to mind the last time you were with the person you are mourning. Contemplate the following questions:

How could anything have been different?

What do I wish I had done that I didn't do?

What would have made a difference in the way I am feeling now?

Visualize yourself and this person interacting. See a pleasant exchange between the two of you. Now say or do whatever it is that you wish you had done at that time. Whether it is granting or asking for forgiveness, holding the person close, expressing your true feelings, or just taking time to listen, do it now. Visualize this scenario as clearly as possible with all the details necessary to make it real. Hold this view for a few moments. Put this vision in a bubble of light. Send this visualization, wrapped in white light energy, into the ethers. Now read the following declaration:

> **Heavenly Mother, I am ever grateful for this opportunity to revisit this situation. I know I must release any hurt feelings, guilt, or resentment I have harbored in the past. To hold on to these emotions cannot bring me happiness or relief. I will no longer allow the past to make my spirit weary with grief. Nothing positive is gained from regrets. The soul of (name) knows how I feel. As I visualized how I wished things had been, I know he/she saw what I saw, felt what I felt, and understood. I know in my heart that we shared love while we traversed the Earth plane and I also understand that we continue to share that love now and forever. Time will erase pain, but nothing will diminish the love. Love is forever.**
>
> **Knowing that (name) is content and at peace in spirit, despite any earthly circumstances to the contrary, makes my heart rest easy. Although separate in the physical, we remain united in spirit and soul. The time has come to let go and move onward to new beginnings. I open my arms and heart wide to receive new joys, blessed events, and grand happenings. I know only the best awaits me now. Thank you, Spirit, for this experience.**

Complete the following exercise. If someone has loaned this ceremony to you, use a tablet to write the questions and answers.

Journal Entries

I fondly remember when the two of us . . .

The most valuable lesson that I learned from this person was . . .

I will always be grateful for the times we shared because . . .

One of the qualities you possessed that I would like to emulate is . . .

Other thoughts . . .

When you have completed the exercise, begin the process of extinguishing the four candles, starting with the green one, saying:

Balance and harmony are yours. (Extinguish the candle.)

Peace is with you now. (Extinguish the blue candle.)

You are pure love. (Extinguish the pink candle.)

Spirit is with you. (Extinguish the purple candle.)

Now, greet life with peace in your heart

Any private declarations you wish to make would be appropriate now.

Ring the bell three times to conclude the ceremony.

Saying Goodbye

If someone near and dear to you is in the process of making their transition, please take this opportunity to say goodbye now. When we are aware someone's passing is imminent, we are being given a blessed occasion to say our goodbyes, leaving nothing unsaid or hanging.

I would also encourage you to ask questions about other family members who have already passed away. I often wish that when my mother was slowly making her exit from this world that I had asked her more about her childhood, her mother and grandmother, or had her repeat some of the humorous stories my father used to tell about the days he spent in the army. No one is left in my family who can answer these questions for me.

One of my cousins was wise enough to tape conversations he had with his great aunt before she passed. She related to him many names of relatives long passed, which helped him with his genealogy work. He will always treasure those tapes. Remember, once these people are gone, the information they possess will no longer be available to you.

In our bustling society so many things happen suddenly, especially death. In the beat of a heart, a loved one can be taken from us, making us wish we had had the time to say goodbye. Make this a special moment so they may be released into the spirit world knowing they are loved. This is a chance to make amends and ask for or extend forgiveness so there are no guilty feelings remaining in either one of you, and no one is left wishing, "If only I had . . ." If the person is comatose or incoherent, speak the words anyway, as if they were hearing and understanding everything that is being said—because on some level of their being, they do hear, they do understand.

The following ceremony is designed to aid in the healing process after the passing of a loved one and should be read in its entirety prior to conducting it. Please gather these tools:

1. A special incense that represents cleansing, healing, and purification, such as myrrh, frankincense, or lavender.
2. Choose a green candle for healing; a white one for purity and cleansing; pink for love; and purple for spirituality.

3. Citrine, diamond, fluorite, garnet, jet, lapis, malachite, moonstone, rock crystal, rose quartz, snow quartz, and tourmaline. Use all the stones or as many as you have in your possession. Wear them or place them on the altar.
4. A dish of salt.
5. A dish of water.
6. A religious symbol, worn or placed on the altar.
7. A photograph of the person, placed on the altar.
8. A small bell.
9. A journal and a pen.
10. A box of tissues.

After preparing yourself according to the manner described previously in this chapter, play soft music, ring the bell three times, and light the incense. Standing in front of the altar, inhale the incense deeply into your lungs several times and fan the smoke onto your being. Begin to light the four candles, starting with the green one. After lighting the green candle, say:

> **I light this candle to help in the healing of my emotions and spirit.**

Light the white candle and say:

> **As I light the white candle, I open myself to the cleansing and purifying of my being.**

Light the pink candle and say:

> **Lighting the pink candle symbolizes my love for (name).**

And light the purple candle, saying:

> **With the lighting of the purple candle, I bring spiritual energy into this ceremony.**

Sit comfortably on the floor or chair in front of the altar. Gaze at the photograph on the altar of the person you mourn. If there are tears, let them flow. Tears cleanse our emotions and help wash away the pain. When you are ready, close your eyes and take several deep breaths, filling your lungs completely, and exhaling through your mouth. Visualize a brilliant white light directly over your head. See it as the brightest light you have ever seen, glowing like a diamond in the sun. Notice the streams of light extending downward onto the top of your head. See and feel this light energy as it touches your crown. Continue feeling and seeing this healing, radiant light energy as it slowly flows down your face and head to your shoulders, back, and chest, down into your trunk area, and flowing into your lower body. Visualize the white light energy forming a bubble of healing light all around your physical body. Sit for a moment within the healing light, soaking in the rays of hope, happiness, healing, and harmony. Begin to read the ceremonial prayer:

> **Father, Mother, God, I ask that the highest and purest blessings be bestowed upon the soul of (name). Her/his time on Earth is complete and it is now the beginning of a new life, a life in spirit. (Name)'s days will now be spent in spiritual growth and understanding. I know her/his lessons were many while in the physical body, and that these lessons will further the soul's growth on the other side of life. I rest easy in the knowledge that she/he is safe and receiving comfort within Spirit's loving embrace. I place my trust in the power of love, knowing that all is well and that her/his soul is at peace. Amen.**

Bring your attention to the green candle flame. Study the flame for a moment and then read the following declaration:

> **I am healed in the knowledge that my friend (mother, father, sister, cousin, etc.) is at peace. There is no more pain, adversity, grief, or stress to deal with. Peace fills that spirit's being and permeates the soul with love. I sigh with relief that peace and plenty**

are hers/his now and rest easy knowing that she/he deserves and has received the highest and the best at last. She/he is forever healed of illness and injury and no longer feels pain, and for this I am eternally grateful. Thank you, Spirit.

Focus your attention on the white candle flame for a moment and then read this statement:

My emotions are cleansed of guilt because we were given the opportunity to express our thoughts and feelings. Things that might have been left unsaid were spoken. What might have been left undone was completed. I am content in the knowledge that (name) was able to hear my expression of love and respect for her/him before she/he passed to spirit, and am grateful for the time to make my feelings known. I can rest easy now knowing that we shared a goodbye.

Be aware of the pink candle flame and make the following declaration:

Love is eternal, love never ends. I know that (name) will love me forever and always, as will I love her/him forever and always. Love knows no boundaries and has no limits. Love can reach between two worlds, uniting one soul to the other. I only need to think of (name) to feel that love from her/him. Her/his love is ever-present. I can take (name)'s love with me wherever I go. Her/his loving spirit is now portable, and knowing this brings me great comfort. I know (name) will shine her/his love energy upon my spirit whenever I feel an extra need for comfort during my Earth journey. When life becomes heavy and I require her/his love energy to see me through, I need only ask for this special blessing. All my days are filled with love, forever and always.

Finally, focus your attention on the flame of the purple candle. Recite the following declaration:

> **My spirit has grown from this experience. I harbor no animosity, guilt, blame, or fear, thanks to the knowledge that dwells within my heart. I touch this spiritual oasis within and receive immediate satisfaction for my present need. God loves me, God loves (name), and for this knowledge, I am eternally grateful. I know we are separate, but yet not apart. (Name) will dwell within my heart always. I can speak to her/him whenever I so desire. I can feel that special love whenever I wish. We are gently bonded together with the twine of spiritual love and captured for all eternity within the loving embrace of God. I give great and humble thanks from every part of my being for the time (name) and I have spent together, knowing we will be enjoined again one day. Thank you, Spirit, for this opportunity to grow spiritually.**

Continue to the journal exercise.

Journal Entries

I will always love (name) because . . .

I am not angry at this parting now because I understand . . .

(Name) taught me to . . .

(Name) touched my life in the following ways:

I will always be grateful for the time . . .

I know (name) loved me because . . .

One special endearing action (name) did was . . .

The way I can continue (name)'s expression of life is by . . .

Extinguish the candle flame in each of the candles, beginning with the green one. After the flame is put out, make the following statement:

Thank you, God, for this healing.

Extinguish the white candle and say:

Thank you, God, for this cleansing.

Extinguish the pink candle and say:

Thank you, God, for the love we shared.

Extinguish the purple candle and say:

Thank you, God, for the spiritual wisdom I have received.

Ring the bell three times to conclude the ceremony.

Journaling can be very beneficial in the healing process and I encourage you to continue to express those feelings that occur in the next few weeks in writing. The words that you express may also comfort you when read in the future, should sadness return. They also could become a nostalgic memory of the departed loved one that you will treasure in years to come.

Go with joy and love in your heart

Affirmations for Passing Over

I am serene in the knowledge that (name) is at peace

Love and laughter fill my heart when I remember (name)

I rest easy in the knowledge that (name)
watches over me from spirit

Happiness is mine knowing I have experienced love

My soul grows stronger with the knowledge of continuous life

Spirit guides me during this time of growth

Conclusion

I sincerely hope this book has been helpful for you thus far in your life's journey and that it will continue to be of assistance to you as you change and grow. My purpose for writing this book was to give women a greater appreciation for who they are and who they are becoming. It was meant to provide rituals to celebrate life in all its forms and ceremonies that would present brighter outlooks during stressful times. My sincere hope is that by performing some of these ceremonies and completing the journaling exercises, you have experienced a change in attitude and discovered a new perception by transforming those perceived lemons into lemonade! Please share your experiences from this book with me.

Many blessings!

Elizabeth Owens

e-mail: celebrate_@yahoo.com

☽ REACH FOR THE MOON

Llewellyn publishes hundreds of books on your favorite subjects!
To get these exciting books, including the ones on the following pages, check your local bookstore or order them directly from Llewellyn.

Order by Phone

- Call toll-free within the U.S. and Canada, 1–800–THE MOON
- In Minnesota, call (651) 291–1970
- We accept VISA, MasterCard, and American Express

Order by Mail

- Send the full price of your order (MN residents add 7% sales tax) in U.S. funds, plus postage & handling, to:

Llewellyn Worldwide
P.O. Box 64383, Dept. K508-8
St. Paul, MN 55164–0383, U.S.A.

Postage & Handling

(For the U.S., Canada, and Mexico)

- $4.00 for orders $15.00 and under
- $5.00 for orders over $15.00
- No charge for orders over $100.00

We ship UPS in the continental United States. We ship standard mail to P.O. boxes. Orders shipped to Alaska, Hawaii, the Virgin Islands, and Puerto Rico are sent first-class mail. Orders shipped to Canada and Mexico are sent surface mail.

International orders: Airmail—add freight equal to price of each book to the total price of order, plus $5.00 for each non-book item (audio tapes, etc.).

Surface mail—Add $1.00 per item.

Allow 2 weeks for delivery on all orders.
Postage and handling rates subject to change.

Discounts

We offer a 20% discount to group leaders or agents. You must order a minimum of 5 copies of the same book to get our special quantity price.

Free Catalog

Get a free copy of our color catalog, *New Worlds of Mind and Spirit*. Subscribe for just $10.00 in the United States and Canada ($30.00 overseas, airmail). Many bookstores carry *New Worlds*—ask for it!

Visit our website at www.llewellyn.com for more information.

Celebrating the Crone
Rituals and Stories

Ruth Gardner

There is an international movement by women aged 56 and older to assert themselves—to be more than a television-watching granny. They are celebrating their age, and the wisdom and experience that come with it.

Throughout history, the passage into Cronehood has been ritualized. In many cultures, the Crone was welcomed as the revered elder of the circle. Ritual is the oldest and most successful method of experiencing truth in a deeply meaningful way.

Celebrating the Crone is for those women who want to experience the power of a personal aging ritual. You will find guidelines for conducting your own Croning ceremony, and you will see the many different ways that other modern women have chosen to honor the spirit of the wise one within.

Embrace the silver hairs, the wrinkles, the change of life. Grab your friends, bring a copy of this book, and celebrate your rite of passage from Maiden to Mother to glorious Crone.

1-56718-292-5
240 pp., $5\frac{3}{16}$ x 6, illus. **$12.95**

To order, call 1-800-THE MOON
Prices subject to change without notice

21 Ways to Attract Your Soulmate

Arian Sarris

Are you ready to meet your true love?

Do you desire to feel a deep, loving connection with someone? Do you want to find a relationship that works, one that makes you feel complete? Do you have the feeling that the right person for you is out there, somewhere?

You can't easily bring in your soulmate just by wishing. You need to light up like a Christmas tree, so the right one can't miss you! How you do that is the purpose of this book. First you will learn what a soulmate is, and the two kinds of soulmates. You will discover how to clear out the old to let in the new, and how to summon the help of your Higher Self and your angels. The book contains 21 exercises designed to help you dream your soulmate into reality, change the magnetic attraction of your aura, cut the cords of old relationships, create a soulmate talisman, and many more visualizations, affirmations, and spells.

1-56718-611-4
264 pp., 5 3/16 x 6 **$9.95**

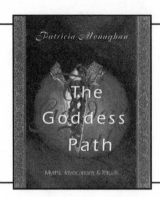

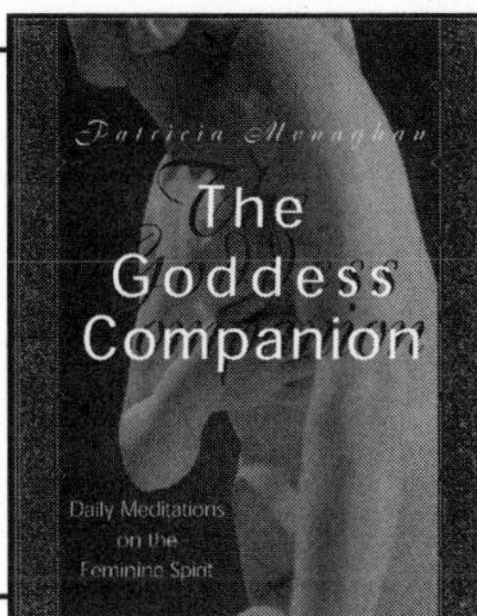

Goddess Companion

Daily Meditations on the Feminine Spirit

Patricia Monaghan

Engage your feminine spirit each day of the year! Here are hundreds of authentic goddess prayers, invocations, chants, and songs—one for each day of the year. They come from dozens of sources, ranging from the great classical European authors Ovid and Horace, to the marvelously passionate Hindu poets Ramprasad and Ramakrishna, to the anonymous gifted poets who first composed the folksongs of Lithuania, West Africa, and Alaska. In fresh, contemporary language that maintains the spirit of the originals, these prayers can be used for personal meditation, for private or public ritual, or for your own creative inspiration. They capture the depth of feeling, the philosophical complexity, and the ecological awareness of goddess cultures the world over.

Organized as a daily meditation book, *The Goddess Companion* is also indexed by culture, goddess, and subject, so you can easily find prayers for specific purposes. Following each prayer is a thoughtfully written piece of prose by Patricia Monaghan which illustrates the aspects of the Goddess working in our everyday lives.

- A perpetual calendar with a daily reading on each page—366 in all
- Includes prayers from Greece, Rome, North and South America, Lithuania, Latvia, Japan, Finland, Scandinavia, India, and many others
- In translations that fully reveal their beauty, making them immediately accessible and emotionally powerful
- Locate goddess prayers by culture, subject, and goddess names

1-56718-463-4

312 pp., 7½ x 9⅛ **$17.95**

To order, call 1-800-THE MOON

Prices subject to change without notice

Goddess Meditations

Barbara Ardinger, Ph.D.

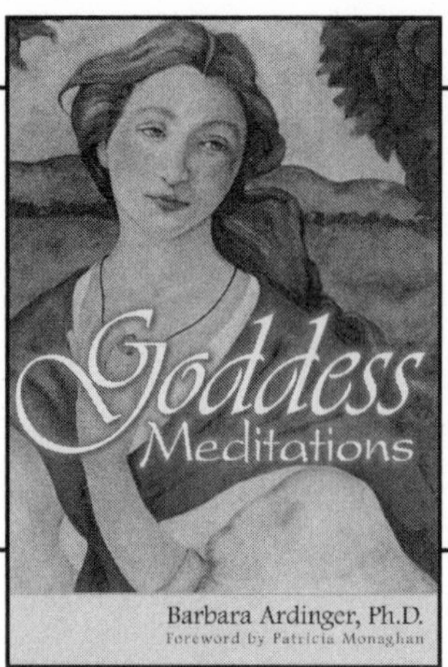

Bring the presence of the Goddess into your daily spiritual practice with *Goddess Meditations,* a book of seventy-three unique guided meditations created for women and men who want to find a place of centeredness and serenity in their lives, both alone and in groups, either in rituals or informally.

Call on a Hestia for a house blessing . . . the White Buffalo Calf Woman for help in learning from your mistakes . . . Aphrodite for love and pleasure . . . Kuan Yin for compassion. Although it's directed toward experienced meditators, this book includes guidelines for beginners about breathing, safety, and grounding, as well as instructions for rituals and constructing an altar.

Also featured is the powerful "Goddess Pillar Meditation," based on the Qabalistic Middle Pillar Meditation; nine Great Goddess meditations that address issues such as protection, community, and priestess power; and seven meditations that link goddesses to the chakras.

1-56718-034-5
256 pp., 7 x 10 **$17.95**

To order, call 1-800-THE MOON
Prices subject to change without notice

Celebrate your life!